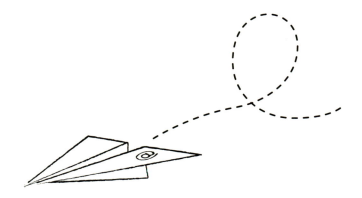

そのまま使える
経理の
英文メール

新日本有限責任監査法人 編

中央経済社

刊行にあたって

　本書は，アーンスト・アンド・ヤング・グローバル・リミテッドのメンバーファームである新日本有限責任監査法人が，グローバル・ファームとしての利点ならびに会計プロフェッショナルとしての知識・経験を生かし，経理財務部門の皆さまへお届けする実用的な英文メールの例文集です。

　環境変化が激しいグローバル社会の中で，企業経営には迅速で的確な経営判断が求められています。また，日本企業においてもグローバル化が急速に進む中で，言葉の壁や商慣習の違いなどを起因とするコミュニケーション上の課題が生じています。特に，海外拠点と密接にコミュニケーションをとる経理財務部門においては適時に正確な情報を迅速に伝達・収集するスキルが求められています。英語での電子メールのコミュニケーションは電話などと比較した場合，より時間の制約の少ない方法ではありますが，これをコミュニケーション上の「小さな課題」と感じている方が多いと思います。新日本有限責任監査法人は，日々クライアントの皆さまの課題解決の支援を行っております。本書は読者の皆さまが抱える，日本人だからこそ，経理財務部門だからこその「小さな課題」を解決することを目指して執筆されました。忙しい皆さまのお手元に置いて，「カット・アンド・ペースト」感覚で「そのまま使って」いただくことを想定し，引きやすさ，使いやすさにこだわった構成としています。

　本書がグローバル社会の最前線に立たれる経理財務部門の皆さまのお役に立つ書となれば幸いです。

　最後になりますが，本書の執筆・編集に際し多大なるご尽力をいただいた中央経済社の末永芳奈氏に心より御礼申し上げます。

平成27年11月

新日本有限責任監査法人

理事長　英　公一

目　　次

Chapter I　本書の使い方　　1

Chapter II　メールの定型文　　9
　　　　　　　－覚えておくと便利なフレーズ

1 件名・冒頭・締め　*10*

2 自己紹介・他人紹介　*20*

3 連絡・日程調整　*25*
　　1　会議の日程調整　*25*
　　☕ 時差や祝日の把握　*29*
　　2　会議の日程・時間・場所の変更・キャンセル　*30*
　　3　会議内容の連絡　*32*
　　4　会議・出張の事前準備　*35*
　　5　事務所移転等の連絡　*36*
　　6　異動・組織変更の連絡　*38*

4 知っていると便利なフレーズ　*40*
　　1　感謝の気持ちを伝えるとき　*40*
　　2　賞賛するとき　*42*
　　3　お祝いを伝えるとき　*43*
　　4　お詫びをするとき　*45*
　　5　クレームを言うとき　*47*
　　6　注意を促すとき　*49*
　　7　期限・督促に関係する表現　*51*
　　8　添付ファイル・メールに関係する表現　*53*
　　9　定型的な言い回し　*56*
　　10　その他の便利なフレーズ　*60*
　　☕ 英語にはない日本語表現　*61*

Chapter Ⅲ　基本となる言い回しの「型」　　63

1　〜についてご連絡します。　*64*
2　〜へご連絡下さい。　*64*
3　〜までに連絡下さい。　*64*
4　〜について質問があります。　*64*
5　〜についてご確認願います。　*64*
6　〜という理解でよろしいでしょうか。　*64*
7　〜はどういう意味ですか？　*64*
8　〜は完了していますか？　*64*
9　どちらを〜でしょうか？　*64*
10　誰に〜でしょうか？　*65*
11　どこを〜でしょうか？　*65*
12　何を〜でしょうか？　*65*
13　〜を予定しています。　*65*
14　〜について変更があります。　*65*
15　〜に決定しました。　*65*
16　〜が利用可能になります。　*65*
17　〜に伝えて下さい。　*65*
18　〜を全員で共有して下さい。　*65*
19　〜を周知徹底して下さい。　*66*
20　〜を作成して下さい。　*66*
21　〜を送付して下さい。　*66*
22　〜の資料を提出して下さい。　*66*
23　〜を添付して下さい。　*66*
24　〜を修正して下さい。　*66*
25　〜に入力して下さい。　*66*
26　〜を入手して下さい。　*66*
27　〜を回覧して下さい。　*66*
28　〜の承認を，〜（人）にもらって下さい。　*66*
29　〜の署名・承認印がありません。　*66*
30　〜について説明して下さい。　*67*
31　〜の理由を教えて下さい。　*67*
32　〜（数値）の内訳を教えて下さい。　*67*
33　〜の見解を教えて下さい。　*67*

34 ～の所要時間を教えて下さい。　*67*
35 ～の頻度を教えて下さい。　*67*
36 ～に従って下さい。　*67*
37 ～（期限）を遵守して下さい。　*67*
38 ～（提出物等）の期限が過ぎています。　*67*
39 ～（マニュアル・データ等）をご参照下さい。　*67*
40 ～のフォローアップをお願いします。　*68*
41 ～について状況の報告をお願いします。　*68*
42 対応して下さい。　*68*
43 ～（の資料）が足りません。　*68*
44 ～（計算シート等）にエラーがあります。　*68*
45 ～と～が一致しません。　*68*
46 ～と～が整合しません。　*68*
47 ～について乖離があります。　*68*
48 ～の計上区分を教えて下さい。　*68*
☕ メールが長すぎない？　ポイントを押さえたメールの記載　*69*

Chapter Ⅳ　場面別　メール表現　71

1 子会社，取引先等への連絡・依頼・回答　*72*

1　売上に関する連絡・依頼・回答　*72*
Case1　第1四半期の売上高を報告してもらう　*72*
Case2　契約書のコピーを送付してもらう　*73*
Case3　取引先の決済条件について確認してもらう　*74*
Case4　販売実績を販売システムへ登録してもらう　*75*
Case5　売上関連証憑の提出遅延を知らせる　*76*

2　購買に関する連絡・依頼・回答　*77*
Case6　請求書を経理部へ送付してもらう　*77*
Case7　仕入先から相見積りを入手してもらう　*78*
Case8　原材料の購入実績を教えてもらう　*79*
Case9　購買申請書に数量誤りのあることを知らせる　*80*
Case10　購買システムと会計システムが連動していることを知らせる　*81*

3　入出金に関する連絡・依頼・回答　*82*
　　Case11　顧客からの入金額と請求額の不一致を知らせる　*82*
　　Case12　送金を至急取り消してもらう　*83*
　　Case13　代金の振込を依頼する　*84*
　　Case14　入金が確認できたことを連絡する　*85*
　　Case15　支払期日を変更してもらう　*86*

4　人件費（その他）に関する連絡・依頼・回答　*87*
　　Case16　新しい給与規定に基づき給与計算を行ってもらう　*87*
　　Case17　賞与額算定の前提条件を教えてもらう　*88*
　　Case18　税務申告書の提出を促す　*89*
　　Case19　不正行為に関する社内の調査結果を教えてもらう　*90*
　　Case20　顧問弁護士の見解を入手してもらう　*91*

5　予算に関する連絡・依頼・回答　*92*
　　Case21　予算の提出を早めてもらう　*92*
　　Case22　売上予算のセグメント別データをメールで送ってもらう　*93*
　　Case23　予算と実績の差異について分析してもらう　*94*
　　Case24　予算達成率を報告してもらう　*95*
　　Case25　来年の購買予算を作成してもらう　*96*

6　決算に関する連絡・依頼・回答　*97*
　　Case26　当期のパッケージ提出スケジュールを知らせる　*97*
　　Case27　パッケージフォームの変更を知らせる　*98*
　　Case28　特定のフォームについて提出する必要のない旨を知らせる　*99*
　　Case29　月次決算での為替レートについて知らせる　*100*
　　Case30　連結システムの入力期限について知らせる　*101*

7　内部統制に関する連絡・依頼・回答　*102*
　　Case31　売上プロセスに係るフローチャートを作成してもらう　*102*
　　Case32　人件費プロセスに係る統制テストを実施してもらう　*103*
　　Case33　統制不備に関する要約表を送ってもらう　*104*
　　Case34　購買プロセスに係るリスクの見直しを行ってもらう　*105*
　　Case35　承認済みの全社統制チェックリストを送ってもらう　*106*

2 子会社，取引先等への質問・回答　107

1　売上に関する質問・回答　107
- **Case36**　請求書の発行担当者について問い合わせる　107
- **Case37**　顧客の与信情報を確認したかどうかについて問い合わせる　108
- **Case38**　顧客への支払督促の頻度について問い合わせる　109
- **Case39**　売上取引の根拠資料の有無について問い合わせる　110
- **Case40**　売上計上の遅れの理由を確認する　111

2　購買に関する質問・回答　112
- **Case41**　購買依頼申請書の内容に関して質問する　112
- **Case42**　発注数量の誤りの可能性について問い合わせる　113
- **Case43**　購買仕訳の入力者に関する理解を確認する　114
- **Case44**　移転価格を考慮しているかどうかについて問い合わせる　115
- **Case45**　関係会社残高確認の差異分析結果を送ってもらう　116

3　入出金に関する質問・回答　117
- **Case46**　送金が完了しているかどうかについて問い合わせる　117
- **Case47**　送金に関する法律上の制限の有無について確認する　118
- **Case48**　支払条件について質問する　119
- **Case49**　口座番号を確認する　120
- **Case50**　送金の内訳について問い合わせる　121

4　人件費（その他）に関する質問・回答　122
- **Case51**　給与テーブルの変更の有無を確認する　122
- **Case52**　弁護士の見解の入手の有無について問い合わせる　123
- **Case53**　税務調査の指摘事項に関する見解について問い合わせる　124
- **Case54**　移転価格税制に関する事前確認が完了しているかどうかについて問い合わせる　125
- **Case55**　監査人による監査が終了していない理由を確認する　126

5　予算に関する質問・回答　127
- **Case56**　予算案が取締役会で承認されたものかどうかについて確認する　127
- **Case57**　予算に対する実績の進捗状況について問い合わせる　128
- **Case58**　売上高を増やす余地の有無について問い合わせる　129
- **Case59**　売上高が下回っている原因について問い合わせる　130

Case60 レポーティングパッケージの入力内容が一致しない理由について問い合わせる　*131*

6　決算に関する質問・回答　*132*
　Case61 繰延税金資産残高の増加理由について問い合わせる　*132*
　Case62 修正仕訳を入力してよいかどうか確認する　*134*
　Case63 棚卸資産の実地棚卸が必要かどうか確認する　*135*
　Case64 引当金の見積りに使用した前提条件について問い合わせる　*136*
　Case65 その他費用に何が含まれているかについて問い合わせる　*137*

7　内部統制に関する質問・回答　*138*
　Case66 社内規定等を変更したかどうかを確認する　*138*
　Case67 内部統制の不備の改善方法について問い合わせる　*139*
　Case68 テスト結果の文書化が完了しているかどうかについて問い合わせる　*140*
　Case69 コントロールの内容について説明してもらう　*141*
　Case70 チェックマークの意味について問い合わせる　*142*

☕ はい／いいえ　英語と日本語の返答の違い　*143*

3 子会社，取引先等へのクレーム・対応　*144*

1　売上に関するクレーム・対応　*144*
　Case71 請求書の金額等の誤りを指摘する　*144*
　Case72 売上伝票等の遅れについて指摘する　*145*
　Case73 出荷の遅れについて指摘する　*146*
　Case74 売上帳の締めの遅れについて確認する　*147*
　Case75 売掛金残高明細のセルフチェックを依頼する　*148*

2　購買に関するクレーム・対応　*149*
　Case76 購買依頼書等の処理の遅れを指摘する　*149*
　Case77 値引等の承認エビデンスがないことを指摘する　*150*
　Case78 検収登録されていない資産について指摘する　*151*
　Case79 注文書等の紛失について連絡する　*152*
　Case80 納品期限等の遅れに対するベンダーへのクレーム　*153*

3　入出金に関するクレーム・対応　*154*

- Case81　売掛金等の回収遅延について対応を依頼する　*154*
- Case82　請求書等と出金額の不一致について指摘する　*155*
- Case83　経費等の支払催促に対する対応を依頼する　*156*
- Case84　入金遅延への対応を依頼する　*157*
- Case85　出金規定等の社内ルールの再検討を依頼する　*158*

4　人件費（その他）に関するクレーム・対応　*159*

- Case86　時間外労働の承認が確認できないことを指摘する　*159*
- Case87　給与等の支払超過への対応を依頼する　*160*
- Case88　依頼資料の送付を督促する　*161*
- Case89　重大なクレーム等の連絡を依頼する　*162*
- Case90　従業員等の処分について連絡する　*163*

5　予算に関するクレーム・対応　*164*

- Case91　差異分析の誤りを指摘する　*164*
- Case92　入力漏れ・エラーについて指摘する　*165*
- Case93　交際費等，費用の大幅増加について指摘する　*166*
- Case94　上長の承認漏れについて指摘する　*167*
- Case95　クレームに対して謝罪する　*168*

6　決算に関するクレーム・対応　*169*

- Case96　連結パッケージの提出遅延について指摘する　*169*
- Case97　会計基準からの逸脱を指摘する　*170*
- Case98　会計方針の変更の事前連絡を依頼する　*171*
- Case99　決算スケジュールの徹底を依頼する　*172*
- Case100　他部門との連携を強化する　*173*

7　内部統制に関するクレーム・対応　*174*

- Case101　職務分掌上の問題点を指摘する　*174*
- Case102　統制テスト手法の相違を指摘する　*175*
- Case103　証憑の未提出を指摘する　*176*
- Case104　統制の不備是正への対応を依頼する　*177*
- Case105　テスト証憑の準備について連絡する　*178*

INDEX　*179*

Chapter I
本書の使い方

Chapter I 本書の使い方

　英文でのコミュニケーションは様々な場面で必要であり，コミュニケーションの内容こそ違えど，職階に関係なく必要なスキルであると言えます。その一方で，ビジネスで使う英文コミュニケーションを教育の場でしっかりと学んだ人は少ないのではないでしょうか。ソーシャル・ネットワーキング・サービスの普及に伴い，若い世代では英語でのコミュニケーションに抵抗感を感じない人も比較的多いと聞きますが，失敗の許されないビジネスでのコミュニケーションとなると日本語だと1分で書くことができる文書が10分以上かかってしまうというケースもよく耳にします。インターネットや書籍で広く情報が収集できる環境にあるにもかかわらず，です。

　これは，日本語でのコミュニケーションと異なり，自分が学んだ，あるいはインターネット等で見つけた表現が若干自分の意図するものと違っていたり，あるいはそれを使用することにより，相手にどういう伝わり方をするかが分からないため，応用が利かず，慎重になってしまうことが原因だと考えられます。親会社を代表して海外子会社に指示を出す局面では，よりレベルの高い文章を送らなければならない，という意識も働くでしょう。他方，日々の忙しい業務の中で，可能であればさっさと作って送ってしまいたいと感じることも多いのではないでしょうか。

　つまり，

> そのまますぐに使える実用的な例文

があればそれに越したことはないということです。母国語ではない言語でのコミュニケーションではニュアンスをうまく伝えられないという意識がどうしても残りますが，コミュニケーションが成立するという成功経験を繰り返すことで自信が生まれ，使用した文章が血となり肉となっていくことでその意識も薄まっていくものと思います。

本書では，そのまますぐに使える実用的な例文を収録すべく，以下の工夫を取り入れました。

👍 1．例文の簡素化，複雑な場面設定の排除

例文を複雑化させることにより，使える場面が限定的になることを防ぎました。

👍 2．単語やフレーズの入れ替え表現の充実

例文を簡素化する一方，簡単に入れ替え可能な単語やフレーズを示すことにより，例文の応用の幅を広げました。

👍 3．例文の厳選

文法的には正しくても表現としては使わない不自然な例文を排除し，実用的な例文だけを採用しました。

👍 4．調べやすさの工夫

読者が目的の例文にたどり着きやすいよう冒頭のContentsはわかりやすい区分にまとめました。

また，各Chapterでは以下のような工夫をしています。

メールの定型文（Chapter Ⅱ）

メールの定型文（Chapter Ⅱ）ではメールの件名，冒頭，締めで使用する例文，自己紹介や日程調整に関する例文など，経理業務に特化しない一般的なやりとりに関する例文を収録しています。

また，『注意を促すとき』など，伝えたいこと（アクション）を中心に必要な例文を探すことが可能です。

「了解です」，「お役に立てば幸いです」など，ちょっとした言い回しは『その他の便利なフレーズ』にまとめました。

たとえば……

> シンプルで探しやすい見出しを採用

> 見出しの「会議の日程調整」に関連した，よく使用する例文を複数収録

❶ 会議の日程調整

	日本語	英語
会議の連絡		
1	12月6日の15:00に弊社オフィスで会議を行いたいと考えています。	I would like to have a meeting at our office on December 6 at 15:00.
2	クリスマス休暇が始まる前に会議を実施したいと考えています。	I would like to have a meeting before the Christmas holidays begin.
3	次回のミーティングは12月6日15:00-16:00になります。出席可否を当メールに返信にてご連絡下さい。	This is to inform you that a next meeting has been scheduled for December 6 15:00 to 16:00. Please confirm your attendance by replying to this email.
4	もしご都合がつかないということであれば，3日前までにご連絡頂けますでしょうか？	Could you please let me know by 3 days before if it does not work for you?

基本となる言い回しの「型」(Chapter Ⅲ)

　基本となる言い回しの「型」(Chapter Ⅲ)ではより経理業務に特化した定型的な言い回しをまとめました。その多くは「Ⅳ　場面別メール表現」でもとりあげられているものです。また，「型」を使いこなすことを想定し，例文に採用した「型」の対訳が何であるかをわかりやすく表現しました。

　たとえば……

<!-- 「型」の対応関係をわかりやすく表現 -->

	日本語	英　語
45	**〜と〜が一致しません。**	
	補助簿と総勘定元帳が一致していません。	The sub ledger <u>and</u> general ledger <u>do not reconcile to each other</u>.
46	**〜と〜が整合しません。**	
	前回提出頂いた資料と今回説明頂いた内容は整合していません。	Your explanation <u>is not consistent with</u> the information in the file you provided to us earlier.

　この型をおさえておけば，INDEXの単語を当てはめて，目的に合ったメールを作ることができます。

場面別　メール表現 (Chapter Ⅳ)

　場面別　メール表現 (Chapter Ⅳ) では担当業務によりどのようなコミュニケーション（場面）が多いのかを考え，「連絡・依頼・回答」，「質問・回答」および「クレーム・対応」という伝えたいこと（アクション）を「売上」，「購買」，「入出金」，「人件費（その他）」，「予算」，「決算」および「内部統制」という場面別に整理しました。

　収録されている具体的な例文がイメージできるよう，目次には例文の和訳そのものを入れてあります。各caseでは基本文1文とその展開文を5文収録しました。

　基本文としてシンプルな例文を採用する一方，その一部を置き換えて違った例文を作れるよう，置き換え可能な単語・フレーズもあわせて収録しています。

たとえば……

> 最も基本的な文を基本文として紹介

Case 1 顧客からの入金額と当社の請求額の不一致

基本文

	日本語	英語
1	A社からの入金額と<u>当社の請求額</u>が不一致です。	Cash received from customer A does not agree with <u>the amount we billed</u>.

> 下線部と置き換え可能な単語・フレーズを収録

当社システム上のデータ（the data in our system）
当社予想金額（the amount we expected）
請求金額（invoice amount）

> 基本文をもとに同じ場面で使うことが想定される例文を展開文として収録。

展開文

	日本語	英語
1.1	A社からの入金額と当社の請求額が100円だけ一致しません。	Cash received from customer A does not match with the amount we billed by JPY 100.
1.2	A社からの入金額と当社の請求額が異なっています。	Cash received from customer A differs from the amount we billed.
1.3	A社からの入金額と当社の請求額の不一致は，当月解消しました。	Inconsistency between cash received from customer A and the amount we billed was fixed this month.
1.4	A社からの入金額と当社の請求額の不一致についてフォローアップをお願いします。	Please follow up on the inconsistency between cash received from customer A and the amount we billed.
1.5	A社からの入金額と当社の請求額の不一致について理由を教えて下さい。	Please tell me the reason for the inconsistency between cash received from customer A and the amount we billed.

また，手っ取り早く必要な単語を調べたい，その単語を使った例文を見たいという場合に対応するため，巻末のINDEXも充実させました．是非有効にご活用ください。

　最後に，「お疲れ様です」や「いつもお世話になっております」といった表現は日本語のメールではよく使用されるものですが，英文メールではどのように表現すればよいでしょうか。本書は英語の悩みが全くないネイティブや海外で生まれ育ったいわゆる帰国子女ではなく，英語でのコミュニケーションに苦労しながらもこれを乗り越えてきたメンバーが中心となり，利用者目線でどうしたら使いやすいか，どういう例文が必要なのかを実体験をもとにしながら執筆しました。
　英語環境で育っていない日本人ならではの悩み所もカバーできたと確信しています。皆様の英語の業務に少しでも役立てることができましたら幸いです。

Chapter II

メールの定型文
－覚えておくと便利なフレーズ

　ChapterⅡでは，英文メールの中でも最も基本的な内容を取り上げます。
　メールを構成する上で必要不可欠な表題，冒頭，締めのフレーズをはじめ，自己紹介，日程調整などの，経理業務に限らずあらゆるビジネスの場で使うことが想定される，一般的で使用頻度の高い例文を中心に掲載しています。
　英文メール全般で重要なことは，事務連絡や感情表現などどのようなシチュエーションにおいても，「何（誰）が」「どうなる（である）」かを具体的に明示することです。本Chapterでは，様々な場面で使える応用しやすい定型文を掲載しています。このポイントに留意して，目的や状況に応じて単語を入れ替えるなどして，大いに活用しましょう。

1 件名・冒頭・締め

　メールの件名および冒頭・締めの定型用語です。件名は伝達内容を具体的かつ簡潔に記載することが重要です。冒頭の宛名は相手の性別，人数や肩書によって，また締めのフレーズは相手の立場によって使い分けることが一般的です。

❶ 件　名

	日本語	英　語
提出依頼		
1	連結決算帳票ご提出のお願い	Request for consolidation reporting package
2	売上関連証憑ご提出のお願い	Request for supporting documents of sales transactions
3	株式売買契約書ご提出のお願い	Request for Stock Purchase Agreement 【その他の契約書名等】 資産取得契約書：Asset Purchase Agreement 雇用契約書：Employment Agreement ロイヤルティ契約書：Royalty Agreement ライセンス契約書：License Agreement 賃貸契約書：Lease Agreement／Tenancy Agreement 合併契約書：Merger Agreement 合弁会社設立契約書：Joint Venture Agreement 不動産売買契約書：Purchase and Sale Agreement of Real Estate 委託販売契約書：Consignment Sales Agreement 委任契約書：Delegation Agreement 請負契約書：Service Agreement 再委託請負契約書：Subcontractor Service Agreement 金銭消費貸借契約書：Loan Agreement

		ソフトウェア開発委託契約書：Consignment Agreement for Software Development 労働者派遣契約書：Worker Dispatch Agreement 覚書：Memorandum of Understanding 委任状：Power of Attorney
4	【（期限前）リマインド】連結決算帳票提出依頼の件 【（1回目）督促】連結決算帳票提出依頼の件 【（2回目）督促】連結決算帳票提出依頼の件	【Friendly Reminder】Request for consolidation reporting package 【Reminder】Request for consolidation reporting package 【Second Reminder】Request for consolidation reporting package
確認・実施依頼		
5	連結決算帳票訂正のお願い	Request for corrections to the consolidation reporting package
6	グループ内取引のご確認のお願い	Request for confirmation of intercompany transactions
7	統制テスト実施のお願い	Request to perform test of controls
8	財務数値増減分析実施のお願い	Request for fluctuation analysis of financial reporting
9	【至急】残高確認状回収フォローアップのお願い	【Urgent】Request to follow up collection of confirmation letters
報告依頼・報告		
10	2015年度税務調査結果報告のお願い	Request to report result of the tax inspection for FY 2015
11	内部統制の不備に関する改善状況のご報告のお願い	Request to report the status on remediation of internal control deficiencies
12	予算実績管理体制強化に関する決定のご報告	Announcement regarding reinforcement decision on monitoring of budget against actual

1 件名・冒頭・締め

打ち合わせ等		
13	新規連結子会社に関する打合せ出席のお願い	Invitation to a meeting of the new consolidated subsidiary
14	新プロジェクト検討のためのアポイントの件	Appointment to discuss our new project
15	アポイント日時変更依頼の件	Request to change our appointment date
16	貴社訪問日程についてのご連絡	Notification of schedules of our visit to your office
お礼		
17	ご協力に対する感謝	Thank you for your cooperation
18	お力添えに対する感謝	Thank you for your assistance
19	アドバイスに対するお礼	Thank you for your advice
スケジュール関係		
20	2015年度末連結決算スケジュールのお知らせ	FY2015 year-end closing schedule for consolidation
21	予算会議日程のお知らせ	Notification of the budget meeting schedule
22	会議日程の変更のお知らせ	Notification of change of the XXX meeting schedule
異動・担当者変更・その他		
23	異動のお知らせ	Notification of personnel transfer
24	担当者変更のお知らせ	Notification of change in a person in charge
25	財務諸表作成担当者のお知らせ	Notification of a person in charge for financial reporting
26	メールアドレス変更のお知らせ	Notification of change of email address
27	営業時間変更のお知らせ	Notification of change in office hours
28	棚卸資産評価に関する会計方針の変更のお知らせ	Notification of change in accounting policy for inventory valuation
29	本社事務所移転のお知らせ	Notification of moving of our Headquarters office
30	組織再編のお知らせ	Notification of reorganization

	質　問	
31	売掛金回転率に関する質問	Inquiry about AR turnover ratio
32	売掛金の回収についての質問	Inquiry about AR collection
33	棚卸資産評価に関する質問	Inquiry about inventory valuation
34	資産除去債務の会計処理に関する質問	Inquiry about accounting treatment of asset retirement obligation
35	連結決算帳票間における金額の不一致に関する質問	Inquiry about inconsistent amounts in the consolidation reporting packages
36	出金伝票への経理部長承認に関する質問	Inquiry about approval for disbursement voucher by Accounting Manager
	不　備	
37	請求書金額の不備の件	Regarding an error in invoice
38	注文書番号X-8635の記載内容の不備の件	Regarding an error in the purchase order No.X-8635
	お詫び	
39	会議日程の訂正とお詫び	Apology and correction of meeting schedule
40	会議への出席キャンセルのご連絡とお詫び	Notice and apology for cancellation of attendance to the meeting
41	資料提出遅延のお詫び	Apology for delay in document submission

❷ 冒頭

	日本語	英語
	宛名	
1	ウィルソン様：男性 ・女性（未婚・既婚を問わない） ・氏名から性別が判別できない場合 ・宛名を連名にする場合	Dear Mr. Wilson, ・Dear Ms. Wilson, ・Dear Robin Wilson, Esq. ・Dear Mr. Wilson, Mr. Parker and Ms. Jones,
2	ご担当者様：相手の氏名が不明，男性1名 ・男性1名以上 ・女性1名 ・女性2名以上 ・男性か女性か不明の1名 ・男性複数かつ／または女性複数 ・役職名を宛名にする場合；営業部長様 ・部署名を宛名にする場合；営業部様 （Dearは省略可） ・メールの受け手・担当部署が不明の場合	Dear Sir, ・Dear Sirs, ・Dear Madam, ・Dear Madams, ・Dear Sir／Madam, ・Dear Sirs／Madams, ・Dear Sales Manager, ・Dear Sales Department, ・To whom it may concern,
3	ジェームズさん （社内の相手，親しい相手，何度かやりとりをしている相手）	Hi James-san,
4	各位，皆様	Dear all, Hi all,／Hello everyone,
5	まだご返信頂けていない皆様へ	To those who have not yet responded,
	挨拶	
6	お疲れ様です。	Hi, Helloなどで代用
7	いつもお世話になっております。	Thank you for your emailなどで代用
8	お元気でお過ごしのことと思います。	I hope this email finds you well.
9	いかがお過ごしでしょうか。	Is everything going well with you?

10	ご無沙汰しておりますが，いかがお過ごしですか。	It has been a while since we spoke. How is everything with you?
11	お元気ですか？	How are you doing?
12	良い週末をお過ごしになられましたでしょうか。	I hope you had a nice weekend.
13	新しい職場で順調にお過ごしかと思います。	I hope you are doing well at the new workplace.
14	先日はお目に掛かれてうれしく存じます。	It was my pleasure to meet you the other day.
15	昨日はお電話でお話できてうれしく存じます。	It was nice speaking with you on the phone yesterday.

お礼

16	ご連絡有難うございます。	Thank you very much for your email.
17	お忙しいところに早速ご返信頂き有難うございます。	Thank you very much for your prompt reply in your busy shedule.
18	迅速なご回答有難うございます。	Thank you very much for your prompt response.
19	お問い合わせ有難うございます。	Thank you for your inquiry.
20	依頼資料のご提出を有難うございます。内容を確認し，質問があればご連絡させて頂きます。	Thank you for submitting the document we requested. We will review and revert back with any questions.
21	ニューヨーク出張の際はお世話になり，有難うございました。	Thank you very much for your help during my business trip to New York.

依頼への対応

22	ご依頼の資料をお送り致しますので，よろしくご査収下さい。	Please see attached for the document you requested.
23	先週の会議で宿題とさせて頂いた件につきまして，回答申し上げます。	I would like to answer the question from the meeting last week.

注意・確認

24	注意してお読み下さい。	Please read this carefully.
25	取り急ぎご連絡させて頂いております。	This is just a quick note.（emailの初め・挨拶の後）

1 件名・冒頭・締め

26	私の理解が正しいか確認させて下さい。	Please let me confirm if my understanding is correct.
27	私の勘違いかもしれませんので，誤解があれば指摘して下さい。	Please correct me if I am wrong.
28	ご多忙とは存じますが，（依頼した）書類作成の進捗状況を教えて頂けますか。	I know you are busy, but could you update me on your status of the document preparation?

賞　賛

| 29 | 本社経理部を代表して，あなた方の功績を称えるためにメールをさせて頂いています。 | I am writing to you on behalf of the accounting department of the headquarters to express its appreciation on your accomplishment. |

❸ 締め

	日本語	英語
	結　語	
1	よろしくお願い致します。 ・目上の人に対して ・フォーマル ・一般的・フォーマル ・一般的 ・一般的・カジュアル ・カジュアル ・お礼状で謝意をこめて使う	Best regards, ・Respectfully,／Respectfully yours, ・Faithfully,／Faithfully yours, ・Truly yours,／Very truly yours ・Sincerely,／Sincerely yours, ・Regards,／Best regards,／Kind regards, ・All the best,／Best wishes ・Gratefully,／Gratefully yours,
2	お手数をおかけ致しますが，引き続きよろしくお願い致します。	I thank you in advance for your continued support.
3	よろしくお願い致します（お願いをした際に）。	Thank you in advance.
4	ご理解を賜りますよう，よろしくお願い申し上げます。	Thank you for your understanding.
5	ご配慮頂き有難うございました。	Thank you very much for your time and consideration.
6	ご協力のほどよろしくお願い申し上げます。	We greatly appreciate your support／cooperation.
7	私にできることがあればご遠慮なくお知らせ下さい。	If there is anything that I can help you with, please do not hesitate to let me know.
	対応依頼・依頼への回答	
8	後ほど確認の上，ご連絡致します。	Let me check and get back to you later.
9	詳細が決まり次第ご連絡下さい。	Please let me know when the details have been fixed.
10	何か留意事項等ございましたらご教示頂けますと幸甚です。	Please let us know if you have any concerns.
11	お気づきの点がございましたら，ご指摘頂けますと幸いです。	We would be grateful if you share any concerns.

12	万が一資料不足等お気づきの点がございましたら私までご連絡下さい。	Please contact me if you notice anything such as missing document or notes.
13	皆様の貴重なご意見をお寄せ頂けますようお願い申し上げます。	We welcome your comments.
14	2月末までにご対応のほどよろしくお願い申し上げます。	We need your follow up by the end of February.
15	特に急ぎではありませんが、お時間のある時に議事録を作成下さい。	It is no rush but please prepare the minutes when you have time.
16	会議に欠席される方は本日中にご一報頂けますでしょうか。	Please let me know by the end of today if you cannot attend the meeting／event.
17	ご多忙中恐縮ですが、添付書類のご確認のほどよろしくお願い申し上げます。	Please check the document attached at your earliest convenience.
18	ただ今検討中ですので、しばしお待ち頂けますでしょうか。	We may need a little more time as this is in a process of internal consultation.
19	お急ぎの場合は、直接担当者までお電話にてご連絡下さい。	Please call the responsible personnel in case of emergency.
20	個人情報が含まれていますので、当然のことですが、取り扱いには十分にご留意下さい。	Please note that it contains personal information that requires your care in handling.

締めの挨拶		
21	良いお返事をお待ちしております。	I hope to hear good news from you.
22	皆様にもよろしくお伝え下さい。	Please send my kindest regards to all of your colleagues.
23	ご参加下さった皆様によろしくお伝え下さい。	Please give my regards to all participants.
24	それではまた後ほどお会いしましょう。	See you then／later.
25	来週のミーティングでお目に掛かれるのを楽しみにしております。	I look forward to seeing you again at the meeting next week.
26	こちらのオフィスであなたとお会いできるのを楽しみにしています。	We look forward to meeting with you at our office.
27	またご一緒にお仕事をさせて頂く機会があることを楽しみにしています。	I look forward to working with you again.

28	よい週末をお過ごし下さい。	Have a nice weekend.
29	今後ますますのご活躍をお祈り申し上げます。	I wish you continuous success.
30	くれぐれもお体にお気を付け下さい。／ご自愛下さい。	Please take care of yourself.

2 自己紹介・他人紹介

初めてメールを送る相手に自分の役職等を紹介する際に使えるフレーズです。また，円滑な引継のため，自分の後任者をCCに入れて，相手に連絡することもあります。

❶ 自己紹介

	日本語	英　語
	基本的な自己紹介	
1	本社経理部課長の田中太郎と申します。連結決算において資本関連取引を担当しております。 【役職名】* ・最高財務責任者 ・本部長 ・部長 ・課長 ・主任 ・支店長 ・工場長 【担当業務】 ・売上債権 ・仕入債務 ・在庫管理 ・原価計算 ・有形固定資産 ・月次決算 ・貸付金 ・外貨建取引 ・法人税申告書作成 ・移転価格税制 ・内部の財務報告 ・開示作成業務	My name is Taro Tanaka, the manager of the accounting department at the Head Office. I am in charge of capital related transactions for consolidation accounting. ・CFO (Chief Financial Officer) ・General Manager ・manager, controller ・assistant manager ・supervisor ・branch manager ・plant manager ・receivables ・payables ・inventory management ・cost accounting ・PPE (Property, Plant and Equipment) ・monthly closing ・loanreceivables ・foreign currency transactions ・preparation of corporate tax return ・transfer pricing taxation ・internal financial reporting ・preparation of presentations and disclosures of financial statements

＊会社によって異なります。

2	本社財務部に勤務しております。	I work in the financial department at the head office.
3	ABC株式会社の田中太郎と申します。	I am Taro Tanaka of ABC Company.
4	ABC株式会社の経理部に所属しております。	I am in the accounting department of ABC Company.
5	経営企画室で海外子会社の営業成績のレビューを担当しています。	I work in the corporate planning department and am responsible for reviewing operating results of foreign subsidiaries.

経歴の説明

6	私は当社の経理部に主任として5年以上勤務しております。	I have been working as a supervisor in the accounting department of our company for more than five years.
7	私は当社の中国子会社に経理部長として3年間駐在しておりましたので、現地の会計基準に精通しています。	I worked in a subsidiary of our company in China as a controller for three years, so I am familiar with the local GAAP.
8	私は海外の企業で10年以上経理業務に携わってきました。	I have over ten years of experience in accounting in a foreign company.
9	私はカリフォルニア州の米国公認会計士の資格を持っています。	I am a U.S. CPA from the State of California.
10	私は民間企業で5年間経理業務に携わったのち、ABC株式会社へ転職してきました。	I had worked in the accounting department for a private company before joining ABC company.
11	私はこの経理の業務経験があまりないため、ご不便をおかけすることがあるかもしれません。	I do not have much experience in this area of accounting, so I might need your assistance.
12	経理部での勤務期間は長いのですが、原価計算を担当するのは初めてです。	Although I have been working in the accounting department for a long time, it is my first time doing cost accounting.

メールの経緯

13	初めてメールをお送りさせて頂いております。	I am writing to you for the first time.

14	御社のJonesさんよりご紹介頂きました。	I was referred to you by Mr. Jones from your company.
15	本社経理部の後藤さんから，佐藤さんが金融商品会計に詳しいとご紹介を頂きました。	I have heard from Goto-san in the headquarters accounting department that Sato-san is very familiar with the financial instruments accounting.
16	先日御社でお目に掛かった際に名刺を交換させて頂きました。	We have exchanged our business cards when we met at your office.
	状況説明	
17	4月から月次決算担当は私ではなくなりました。	As of April, I am no longer responsible for monthly closing.
18	鈴木さんの業務を私が引き継ぐことになりました。	I will be taking over Suzuki-san's work.
19	今年の5月にこちらの経理部に配属になりました。	I was assigned to the accounting department in May.
20	今年の9月から私が貴社との連絡窓口になります。	I will be your contact from September.
21	私は東京本社からの出向社員です。	I am a secondee from the head office in Tokyo.
22	出向でシンガポール事務所に勤務しております。	I am working at our Singapore office on secondment.
23	ABCに吸収合併されたXYZで働いていました。	I worked at XYZ Company which was merged with ABC Company.
24	吸収合併前は経理部長でした。	I was a manager of accounting department before the merger.
25	昨年の8月に産休から復帰しました。	I returned to work last August after maternity leave.
26	私は東京エリアでの在庫管理の主担当者です。	I am responsible for the inventory management for Tokyo area.
27	日本側でのあなたと同じ役職を担当しています。	I am in the counterpart position of yours at Japan side.

❷ 他人紹介等

	日本語	英語
1	経理部のスタッフで月次決算を担当している鈴木和也をご紹介致します。	I would like to introduce you Mr. Kazuya Suzuki, a staff of the accounting department who is in charge of monthly closing.
2	英語が堪能で，国際財務報告基準について幅広い知識を持っています。	He speaks English fluently and has extensive knowledge of IFRS.
3	彼は以前，横浜倉庫で原価計算を担当していたので，現場の事情をよく知っています。	He used to work in Yokohama warehouse as an in-charge of cost accounting, so he knows the situation of the site well.
4	本件に関するメールを送る際は，必ず鈴木さんをCCに入れるようお願い致します。	Please CC Suzuki-san when you send an email regarding this matter.
5	彼は私と2年半一緒に働いております。	He has been working with me for two and a half years.
6	山田さんと私はよく一緒に仕事をしています。	Yamada-san and I are working closely with each other.
7	私が不在の間は，田中さんに承認権限を委譲します。	I delegated my approval authority to Tanaka-san while I am away.
8	田中さんはこのプロジェクトの主要メンバーですので，ご質問がありましたら彼にご連絡頂けますようお願い致します。	If you have any questions, please ask Tanaka-san who is one of the key members of this project.
9	お問い合わせの件に関しては，このメールのCCにいる阿部さんが担当となります。	I have cc'ed Abe-san, who is in-charge and can answer your questions on this matter.
10	阿部さんから後程連絡するよう手配しておきます。	I will have Abe-san contact you later／shortly.
11	次回からは阿部さんと直接やり取りして頂いて結構です。	From next time, you may contact Abe-san directly.
12	あなたからの質問には彼から回答致します。	He will answer your question.

2 自己紹介・他人紹介

13	あなたからご依頼頂いた情報は彼からお送り致します。	He will provide you with the information you requested.
14	この問題については前任者であるAndyがより情報を持っています。困ったら彼に聞いて下さい。	Andy, the fomer in-charge of this matter, should have more information. If you need help, please ask him.
15	佐藤さんは金融商品会計に詳しいので，この有価証券の会計処理については彼女に相談してみることをお勧め致します。	I recommend that you discuss the accounting treatment for the investment securities with Sato-san because she is very familiar with the financial instruments accounting.

3 連絡・日程調整

日程調整の際には，間違いが生じないように的確に日時や場所を伝えることが求められます。また，諸事情により会議の時間や場所が変更となることもあるため，変更に関するフレーズも紹介します。

❶ 会議の日程調整

	日本語	英 語
会議の連絡		
1	12月6日の15:00に弊社オフィスで会議を行いたいと考えています。	I would like to have a meeting at our office on December 6 at 15:00.
2	クリスマス休暇が始まる前に会議を実施したいと考えています。	I would like to have a meeting before the Christmas holidays begin.
3	次回のミーティングは12月6日15:00-16:00になります。出席可否を当メールに返信にてご連絡下さい。	This is to inform you that a next meeting has been scheduled for December 6 15:00 to 16:00. Please confirm your attendance by replying to this email.
4	もしご都合がつかないということであれば，3日前までにご連絡頂けますでしょうか？	Could you please let me know by 3 days before if it does not work for you?
5	昨日，電話会議は12月9日の午後6時開始とお伝えしましたが，これは日本時間です。ドイツ時間では午前10時開始となります。	Although I told you yesterday that the telecon would start at 6pm on December 9, this meant Japan time. It will start at 10am Germany time.
先方に都合を聞く場合（日時指定あり）		
6	12月6日の15:00に弊社オフィスで会議を行いたいと考えていますが，ご都合はいかがでしょうか？	We would like to have a meeting in our office at 15:00 on December 6. Does that work for you?
7	12月6日の弊社オフィスで会議を設定したいと考えていますが，何時がよろしいでしょうか？	I would like to set up a meeting at our office on December 6. What time would work for you?
8	12月6日の15:00に会議を行いたいと考えていますが，場所はどちらがよろしいでしょうか？	Where would you like to have a meeting at 15:00 on December 6?

9	お手数ですが，12月6日の15:00に弊社オフィスまでお越し頂けますでしょうか？	Could you come to our office on December 6 at 15:00?
10	12月4日のご都合はいかがでしょうか？	How does December 4 work for you?
11	日本時間の18:00-19:00，英国時間の9:00-10:00はいかがでしょうか？	How about 18:00-19:00 Japan time (9:00-10:00 UK time)?
12	私は来週だと水曜日と木曜日であれば都合がいいのですが，いかがでしょうか？	I am available on Wednesday and Thursday next week. Let me know what works best for you.

先方に都合を聞く場合（日時指定なし）

13	弊社オフィスで会議を行いたいと考えていますが，ご希望の日時はありますか？	I would like to have a meeting at our office. When are you available?
14	できる限り早急に電話会議を行いたいのですが，最も早く対応可能な日を教えて下さい。	We would like to have a conference call as soon as possible. Could you please let me know your earliest available date?
15	9月第1週と第2週で都合のよい候補日をいくつか指定して頂けますでしょうか？	Could you suggest available dates (and times) that would be convenient for you in the 1st and 2nd weeks of September?
16	来年度の定例ミーティングのスケジュールを決めてしまいませんか？	Can we decide the dates of regular meetings for next year?

日程についての返答

17	12月4日の15:00以降が都合がいいです。	December 4, after 15:00 is good for me.

スケジュール調整

18	会議の候補日が知りたいので，Outlookのカレンダーの閲覧権限を付与して下さい。	Could you please give me access to your Outlook calendar as I would like to know possible dates of for a meeting?
19	私はあなた方の希望日に会議に出席できるようにスケジュールを調整中です。確定したらご連絡致します。	I will try to arrange my schedule to attend the meeting of your preferred date. I will let you know once it is confirmed.

| 20 | 来週であれば問題ありませんが、よろしければ今週に会議ができるよう調整します。 | Next week works for me. However, if you prefer, I will arrange my schedule so that we can have the meeting this week. |

自分が訪問する場合

| 21 | ミーティングのため来週の火曜日に貴社にお邪魔したいのですが、よろしいでしょうか？ | Would it be possible to have a meeting with you at your office next Tuesday? |
| 22 | 12月6日のミーティングはどちらにお邪魔すればよろしいでしょうか？ | It would be appreciated if you can let me know the place of the meeting on December 6. |

他者の同席を依頼する場合（とその回答）

23	11月10日に電話会議を行いたいと考えていますが、社長はご参加可能でしょうか？	We would like to have a telephone conference on November 10. Will the president be able to attend the meeting?
24	9月4日に貴社を訪問する予定なのですが、社長はその日はご在席でしょうか？	We are planning to visit your office on September 4. Will your president be available to see us on that day?
25	10月第2週に貴社を訪問する予定なのですが、社長のご予定に空きがある日はありますか？	I will come to your office in the 2nd week of October. I would like to ask the availability of the president on that week.
26	主な議題は、今年度の決算方針の確認ですので、貴社CFOおよび財務コントローラーの会議へのご出席を期待しています。	Main purpose (of the meeting) is to confirm／ask about your accounting closing policy for this year; thus, we would like your CFO and Financial Controller (FC) to attend the meeting.
27	CFOと財務コントローラーのスケジュールを調整する必要があるため、12月3日までに会議スケジュールをご連絡下さい。	Please let us know the meeting schedule by December 3, as I need to arrange the schedule of CFO and FC.
28	スケジュールを調整しましたが、今回はCFOは会議に出席できません。	Our CFO will not be able to attend the meeting this time although we tried to arrange his schedule.
29	彼は12月9日の会議に出席する予定です。	He will attend the meeting on December 9.

3 連絡・日程調整

30	CFOの代わりにFCが会議に出席します。	FC will be attending the meeting on behalf of CFO.
31	Paulさんを通訳として電話会議に呼んで下さい。	Please invite Paul-san to the tele conference as a translator.
32	こちらは英語が堪能なメンバーがいないので，日本語への通訳ができる人を会議に参加させてもらえませんか？	At our side, we don't have members who can speak English well. Would it be possible to invite someone to the conference who can translate into Japanese?

遅刻・出席できない連絡

33	明日の電話会議の直前に別の会議が入ってしまいましたので，もしかしたら参加が遅くなるかもしれません。	Since I have another meeting just before the telecon tomorrow, I might be late for joining it.
34	申し訳ありませんが，12月6日は別の急ぎの予定が入ってしまいました。	I am sorry but something urgent came up on 6th December.
35	残念ながら来週の会議には出席できなくなったことをお伝えします。	I regret to inform you that I will not be able to attend next week's meeting.
36	今回の会議の欠席についてご理解いただき，どうもありがとうございます。	Thank you for your understanding that I am not able to attend the meeting this time.

時差や祝日の把握

　日本と時差がある国の方とミーティングなどの日程調整をする際には，お互いの所属するタイムゾーンを意識する必要があります。特に，アメリカ等のように同じ国の中で複数のタイムゾーンを持つ場合や，サマータイム制度を導入している国の場合，留意が必要です。このため，電子メール等でミーティングの時間を設定する際には，以下のような工夫をしてタイムゾーンを明示するようにしましょう。
　日本時間の午後3時：**3 pm JST** や **3 pm Japan time** 等

　また，ミーティングを設定する相手の国の祝日も把握しておくとスムースに進みます。
　例えば，以下のインターネットサイトで各国の祝日を把握することができます。
http://www.timeanddate.com/holidays/

❷ 会議の日程・時間・場所の変更・キャンセル

	日本語	英 語
変　更		
1	先日お伝えした会議の日付に誤りがありました。12月8日ではなく，正しくは12月9日です。	There was an error in the date of the meeting of which I informed you the other day. It is not December 8 but 9.
2	昨日，電話会議はA会議室で行うとお伝えしましたが，A会議室の予約が取れませんでしたので，代わりにB会議室で行うこととなりました。	I told you yesterday that the telecon would be held in the meeting room A. However, as the meeting room A is not available, we will use the meeting room B instead.
3	会議の開始時間を11:00からに変更して頂くことはできますか？	Would it be possible to change the starting time of the meeting from 11:00?
4	会議の開始時間を1時間遅らせることはできますか？	Would it be possible to delay the starting time of the meeting by an hour?
5	会議の開始時間を1時間遅らせることは可能です。	We can delay the starting time of the meeting by one hour.
6	直前のご連絡で申し訳ありませんが，明日の会議は再調整となります。	I apologize for the last minute／late notice, but the tomorrow's meeting will be rescheduled.
7	もし明日のご都合が悪いということであれば，会議を明後日に延期しましょうか？	Shall we postpone the meeting until the day after tomorrow if tomorrow does not work for you?
8	10月に予定していた会議ですが，11月に変更させて頂けますでしょうか？	Is it possible to postpone the meeting to be held in October to November?
9	11月13日は本部長が不在のため，日程変更をお願いできますでしょうか？	Can you reschedule the meeting due to absence of our general manager on November 13?
キャンセル		
10	10月に予定していた会議はキャンセルとさせて頂けますでしょうか。	Would it be possible to cancel the meeting to be held in October?

11	10月に予定していた会議ですが，諸般の事情により開催できなくなりました。ですので，何か質問があればメールで回答します。	We regret to inform you that the meeting in October is cancelled due to various reasons. If you have any questions, please email us and we will get back.
12	12月に予定している会議ですが，日程の調整がつかず，延期となりました。	The meeting to be held in December will be postponed due to schedule conflicts.
13	12月に予定している会議ですが，日程の調整がつかず，延期となる可能性が出てきました。	The meeting to be held in December may be postponed due to schedule conflicts.
14	誠に申し訳ありませんが，問題が発生したため，今すぐ工場へ行く必要があります。今日の会議はキャンセルとさせて頂けないでしょうか？	I'm sorry but a problem occurred and I have to go to a factory now. It would be appreciated if I could cancel the meeting today.

3 連絡・日程調整

❸ 会議内容の連絡

	日本語	英　語
会議の主旨説明等		
1	新しいレポーティングパッケージの説明のため，電話会議を行いたいと考えています。	I would like to set up a conference call in order to explain the new reporting package.
2	取締役会に先立って，実務者レベルでの電話会議を開催したいと考えています。	I think it is useful to have a conference call on the practitioners' level before the board of directors meeting.
3	会議の主旨は，決算早期化についてです。	The main topic of the meeting is how we can accelerate financial closing.
会議の進め方等		
4	会議の冒頭で，皆様に1分間程度で自己紹介をして頂きたいと考えていますので，事前にご準備をお願い致します。	We would like to ask everyone to introduce yourself for one minute at the beginning of the meeting. Please make sure you are prepared.
5	会議が始まるまでに添付の決算留意事項をご一読下さい。	Please read the attachment of items to consider in the financial closing prior to the meeting.
6	当日は添付の議題に沿って会議を進行したいと考えています。	The meeting will be conducted along with the agenda as attached.
7	後ほどOutlookで会議招集をお送りします。	I will send a meeting invitation in Outlook later.
8	電話会議の際にはそちらから+81-XXXに電話して下さい。お電話をお待ちしております。	Please call at +81-XXX for the teleconference. We will be waiting for your call.
9	電話会議の際にはこちらから電話しますので，電話番号や会議ID等を教えて下さい。	We will call you for the teleconference so please let us know your number, conference ID etc.
会議で使用する資料等に関する連絡		
10	第3四半期の決算スケジュールを添付致しますので，よろしくご査収下さい。	Please find the attached schedule for the third quarter closing.

11	明日の会議のアジェンダ（議題）を添付致します。	Please find attached the meeting agenda for tomorrow.
12	明日のアジェンダをドラフトして送付してもらえますか？	Could you draft the meeting agenda for tomorrow and send it to us?
13	アジェンダ（議題）に追加したい項目があれば，遠慮なく私までご連絡下さい。	If you have any topics you wish to add to the agenda, please feel free to let me know.
14	アジェンダ（議題）に新しい収益認識基準に関するディスカッションを追加して頂けますか？	Could you please add a topic about the new revenue recognition rules to the agenda?
15	添付のアジェンダのうち，1点目の「決算スケジュール」について時間をかけて議論したいと考えています。	We would like to focus on the discussion about the "closing schedule", the first item on the attached agenda.
16	会議で使用する資料がありましたら，事前にメールでお送り下さい。	Should you have any documents to use in the meeting, please email us in advance.
17	会議で使用する資料を送ります。出席者に転送して下さい。	I'm sending documents that we would like to use in the meeting. Please forward my email to people who will be joining the meeting.
18	新しい収益認識の会計基準に関する研修資料をお送りします。	I have attached the training material regarding the new accounting standards for revenue recognition.
メールの受け手		
19	会議招集をお送り頂きまして有難うございます。	Thank you for the meeting invitation.
20	ぜひ直接お会いしてこの案件について話し合いたいと思っていますので，会議の招集を了承致します。	Since I would like to discuss this matter with you in person, I accept the invitation.
21	今ちょっとバタバタしているので後ほどご連絡致します。	I will let you know later since I am occupied with other business.
22	第3四半期の決算スケジュールのファイルを送って頂けますか？	Could you send me the 3rd quarter closing schedule?

23	私どもの出席者は3名ですので，資料は3部ご用意頂けますでしょうか？	Since three of us will attend the meeting, will you please prepare three sets of materials?
24	新しい収益認識の会計基準に関する研修資料をお送り頂けますと大変助かります。	We would appreciate it, if you could provide us with training materials on new accounting standards for revenue recognition.

Chapter II

メールの定型文

❹ 会議・出張の事前準備

	日本語	英 語
1	緊急時には直ちに080-XXXX-XXXXにお電話下さい。	In case of an emergency, please call 080-XXXX-XXX immediately.
2	受付で，経理部の田村とアポイントを取っている旨を伝えて下さい。	At the information desk, please let the receptionist know you have an appointment with Tamura of the accounting department.
3	国際ビルの1階の，受付横でお会いしましょう。	I will meet you up at the first floor of the Kokusai building, next to the reception.
4	会議は，5階の5311会議室で行います。	The meeting will take place in the room #5311 on the fifth floor.
5	田中さんと私であなたを空港までお迎えに上がります。荷物を受け取ったら080-XXXX-XXXXにお電話下さい。	Tanaka-san and I will pick you up at the airport. Please call 080-XXXX-XXXX after you pick up your luggage.
6	滞在期間のあなたの宿泊先は私どもの方で手配します。	We will arrange accommodations for you during your stay.
7	IDカードの発行を依頼するので，フルネームと所属を教えて下さい。	May I have your full name and department, so that we can request to issue an ID card?
8	会議へのPCの持ち込みは禁止ですので予めご了承下さい。	Please be informed that you are not allowed to bring your PC to the meeting.
9	入館証を携帯していない場合は建物には入れません。	You cannot enter the building without an entrance card.
10	来社の際は身分証を必ずお持ち下さい。	Please make sure that you bring your ID with you when you come to our company.
11	土曜日は正面玄関が閉鎖されていますのでご注意下さい。	Please note the main entrance is closed on Saturdays.
12	本社建物内は許可された方以外立ち入り禁止です。	Only authorized personnel can enter the headquarters building.

❺ 事務所移転等の連絡

	日本語	英語
1	4月1日付で弊社はオフィスを移転することをご連絡致します。	This is to inform that we will move our office on April 1.
2	4月1日付で弊社はオフィスを大阪から東京に移転しました。	On April 1, we moved our office from Osaka to Tokyo.
3	新しいオフィスの住所をお知らせ致します。	We would like to inform you of the address of our new office.
4	最寄駅は東京駅になります。	The nearest station is Tokyo Station.
5	駅からオフィスまでの道順を添付致します。	Please find attached directions from the station to our office.
6	オフィスの引っ越し作業のため、3月31日は午前中で業務を終了します。	Due to moving our office, we will be closed in the afternoon of March 31.
7	オフィスの引っ越し作業のため、3月31日の午後から4月1日の午前中の間は連絡が取れません。	Due to moving our office, we will not be available from the afternoon of March 31 until the morning of April 1.
8	引っ越し当日はご迷惑をおかけ致しますが、ご理解をお願い致します。	We apologize for any inconvenience this may cause you on the day of the moving. Thank you for your understanding.
9	4月1日の午後からは通常業務に戻る予定です。	We will return to the normal operation on the afternoon of April 1.
10	電話番号に変更はありません。	Telephone number will remain the same.
11	4月1日よりメールアドレスが変更になりますことをお知らせ致します。	This is to inform you that our email addresses will be changed on April 1.
12	新しいeメールアドレスは以下のとおりです。	A new email address is as follows.
13	引き続きご支援よろしくお願い致します。	Thank you for your continuing support.
14	4月1日より連結会計システムのURLが変更になります。	On April 1, URL of the consolidation accounting system will be changed.
15	このたび、ラオスに支店を開設することになりましたので、ご報告致します。	Please be informed that we are opening a branch in Laos.

| 16 | このたび，弊社は事業のグローバル化に対応するために，社名をヤマト産業株式会社からYMT株式会社に変更することになります。 | We are changing the company name from Yamato Industries Co. Ltd. to YMT Co., Ltd. in order to address the globalization of our businesses. |

❻ 異動・組織変更の連絡

	日本語	英 語
1	人事異動でバンコクに転勤することになりましたことをお知らせ致します。	I am writing this email to inform you that I will be transferred to Bangkok.
2	山田さんは今月付で経理部から営業部門に異動になりました。	Yamada-san was transferred from the accounting department to the sales department this month.
3	資金部長は田中さんになります。	Tanaka-san will be the Treasury manager.
4	4月からは鈴木さんが経理本部長になります。	Suzuki-san will be the general manager of the accounting department starting in April.
5	このたび私たちのチームの和田さんが課長に昇進したことをご報告致します。	I would like to inform you that Wada-san from our team was promoted to assistant manager.
6	武田さんは引退され，山下さんがCFOの職務を引き継ぐことになりました。	Takeda-san has retired and Yamashita-san will take over as CFO.
7	彼が経理部長である佐々木さんの後任となります。	He will be replacing Sasaki-san as the financial controller.
8	小川さんが小池さんの業務をサポートすることになりました。	Ogawa-san will support Koike-san's work／tasks.
9	彼が佐々木さんの業務を引き継ぎます。引継ぎは佐々木さんが離れる前の今週中に完了します。	He will take over Sasaki-san's work. The handover will be completed by the end of this week before Sasaki-san leaves.
10	このたびの組織変更で，旧財務部は資金部と経理部に分割されることになりました。	Due to the change of organization, the former finance department will be divided into the treasury department and the accounting department.
11	このたびの組織変更で，経理部と資金2部が統合され，財務部となりました。	Due to the change of organization, the accounting department and the treasury department 2 will be merged and become the finance department.

12	組織再編後の組織図を添付致します。	Please find attached an organization chart after reorganization.
13	新しい組織体制は2015年4月1日から適用となります。	The new organization will be effective on April 1, 2015.
14	12月10日をもって，ABC社を退職することになりました。	I am leaving ABC Company on December 10.
15	私の業務は山田さんが引き継ぐことになっています。	Yamada-san will take over my job.
16	在職中の皆様のサポート，大変感謝しております。	I really appreciate your support while I worked here.
17	ABC社での10年間は非常に刺激的でした。	The 10 years I worked for ABC Company was very exciting.
18	またいつか再会できることを楽しみにしております。	I hope to see you again sometime.
19	退職後はXYZ商事の経理部に勤務することになっています。	I will work in the accounting department of XYZ corporation.
20	ABC社を退職した後の進路は未定です。	I have not yet determined what to do after leaving ABC Company.
21	皆様のますますのご発展をお祈り申し上げます。	I wish you success in the future.

3 連絡・日程調整

4 知っていると便利なフレーズ

相手の協力に対して感謝や謝意を表明することによって,より円滑にコミュニケーションが行えるようになります。ここではビジネスの場面でよく使うフレーズを紹介しています。

❶ 感謝の気持ちを伝えるとき

	日本語	英語
1	迅速にご対応頂き有難うございました。	I really appreciate your prompt action.
2	あなたのご助力に感謝しています。	I am very thankful for your support.
3	引き続きご協力頂き有難うございます。	Thank you very much for your continuous cooperation.
4	詳細なご説明を有難うございます。	Thank you for your detailed explanation.
5	ご協力に本当に感謝しています。	I truly appreciate your help.
6	ご提案頂き有難うございます。	Thank you for your suggestions.
7	質問に対して,早速のご回答を有難うございます。	Thank you very much for your prompt reply to my inquiry.
8	先日は打ち合わせにお時間を頂き有難うございました。	Thank you very much for your time to have the meeting with us.
9	出張時はサポートして頂き有難うございました。	Thank you for your support while I was on business trip.
10	お忙しいところお時間を頂き有難うございました。	Thank you for taking time out of your busy schedule.
11	依頼資料の作成にお時間を割いて頂き有難うございます。	Thank you for taking your time preparing the requested documents.
12	期限内に対応して下さって感謝しています。	Thank you for keeping the deadline.
13	(親しい人に対して) 今日はあなたのお蔭で助かりました。	You saved my day.
14	ここに感謝の気持ちをお伝えさせて頂きます。	I express my sincere gratitude here.

15	皆様のサポートのお蔭で月次決算を終えることができました。	We could finish the monthly closing thanks to your continuous support.
16	そう仰って頂けると大変心強いです。	Those words are very encouraging to me.
17	お褒めにあずかり大変うれしく存じます。	I am greatly flattered by your compliment.
18	私の報告書をお褒め頂いて嬉しく存じます。	I'm glad to receive compliments on my report.
19	この１年間の皆様のご助力とご親切に対する感謝をお伝え致したく、ご連絡させて頂きました。	I am writing this email to show my appreciation for your help and warmhearted kindness throughout this year.
20	あなたの正確で迅速な仕事ぶりにとても感謝しています。	I appreciate your accurate and prompt work.
21	あなたと一緒に働くことのできる素晴らしい機会を持つことができてとても感謝しています。	I am thankful that I have such a wonderful opportunity to work with you.
22	あなた方の協力がなければ，このプロジェクトを終わらせることはできなかったでしょう。	We could not have finished this project without your help.
23	本社／経営陣が皆さんに感謝の気持ちを伝えるようにとのことでした。	The headquarters／management told us they would like to thank you all.
24	田中さんに今度お会いになったら有難うと伝えて頂けますか。	Could you pass my gratitude to Mr. Tanaka when you see him?
25	鈴木さんにも私がお礼を申し上げていたとお伝え下さい。	Please tell Suzuki-san I said thank you.

4 知っていると便利なフレーズ

❷ 賞賛するとき

	日本語	英 語
1	ご一緒にお仕事ができて嬉しく思います。	I am excited to be able to work with you.
2	とても素晴らしい提案です。	Your proposal sounds great.
3	その企画は最高です。	That plan seems terrific.
4	それは名案です。	It is such a great idea.
5	あなたは素晴らしいチームメンバーです。	You are an excellent team member.
6	あなたはとても仕事熱心な人です。	You are such a hardworking person.
7	この作業にあなた以上の適任者はいません。	I could not think of anyone better than you to work on this job.
8	仕事が早いですね。	You get your job done quickly!
9	あなたのレポートは予想以上の出来です。	Your report exceeded my expectations.
10	あなたはチームにとって必須の人材です。	You are the key member of our team.
11	あなたの業績は賞賛に値します。	Your performance is admirable.
12	素晴らしい学歴と職務経験をお持ちですね。	You have a great academic background and job experiences.
13	彼の仕事ぶりは極めて優れています。	His performance is outstanding.
14	あなたならきっと期限内にやり遂げて下さると思っていました。	I was sure you could make it on time.
15	私の知る限り，あなたはわが社の会計システムに最も詳しい人です。	As far as I know, you are the most knowledgeable person regarding our accounting system.
16	時間がない中，完成度の高い文書を作成して下さって有難うございました。	I appreciate that you have prepared such quality documentation under the tight timeline.

❸ お祝いを伝えるとき

	日本語	英　語
1	おめでとうございます！	Congratulations!
2	心の底からお祝いを申し上げます。	I'd like to congratulate you from the bottom of my heart.
3	それを聞いて私も本当に嬉しく思っております。	I am delighted to hear the news.
4	この度はご昇格おめでとうございます。	Congratulations on your promotion.
5	ご昇進されたと聞いて，とても嬉しく思っています。	I am happy to hear that you got promoted.
6	ご昇格のお祝い会をさせて下さい。	Could I host the celebration for your promotion?
7	取締役へのご就任を心よりお祝い申し上げます。	Congratulations on your promotion to an executive director.
8	田中さんへご昇進おめでとうございますとお伝え下さい。	Please give my congratulations to Mr. Tanaka on his promotion.
9	そのプロジェクトのメンバーに選ばれるなんて本当に幸運ですね。	How fortunate you are to be a member of the project!
10	長年の努力が報われましたね。	It looks like all your hard work has finally paid off.
11	大変なご苦労があったことと存じますが，皆様の安堵はいかほどかと推察申し上げます。	I know there had been many difficulties, and I can only imagine how relieved you must be.
12	連結決算が本日完了したことを報告できて本当に嬉しく思います。	I am excited to announce that we have finished the consolidation closing.
13	私たちの企画が採用されたことはとても喜ばしい知らせです。	It is great news that the Company accepted our proposal.
14	案件を獲得したと伺って，大変嬉しく思っています。	I am very glad to hear that you won the projects.
15	５年間連続してわが社の売上が増加していることは本当に喜ばしいことです。	It is great to see that we are constantly growing in the past 5 years in terms of the revenue.

16	創立10周年を迎えられたとのこと、お祝い申し上げます。	I'd like to offer you my congratulations for the 10th anniversary of your company's establishment.
17	新社屋の完成おめでとうございます。貴社の皆様もさぞお喜びのことと存じます。	Congratulations on the completion of your company's new building! I can't imagine how happy you all are.
18	本社を代表してお祝い申し上げます。	I would like to express sincere congratulations on behalf of the headquarters.

❹ お詫びをするとき

	日本語	英 語
1	お詫び申し上げます。	Please accept our apologies.
2	返信が遅くなり申し訳ありません。	I am sorry for the delay in responce.
3	説明不足で申し訳ありません。	Excuse me about my insufficient explanation.
4	間違えて申し訳ありませんでした。	I am sorry for my mistake.
5	誤った資料をお送りしてしまい申し訳ありません。	I am sorry for submitting the wrong documents.
6	提出書類に記載もれがあり，大変申し訳ありませんでした。	I am very sorry that the documents were incomplete.
7	期限に間に合わず申し訳ありません。4月5日までにはマネジメントアカウントを提出します。	I am sorry I missed the deadline. I will submit the management accounts by April 5th.
8	お忙しいところにお邪魔して申し訳ございません。	I am sorry for bothering you when you are busy.
9	ご不便をおかけ致します。	We apologize for the inconvenience.
10	直前のお知らせで申し訳ありません。	I apologize for such short notice.
11	直前でスケジュールが変更となり，ご迷惑をお掛け致します。	We sincerely apologize for the inconvenience caused by the last minute change in the schedule.
12	質問が重複して申し訳ありません。	I am sorry about our duplicated inquiries.
13	申し訳ありませんが，その質問に回答させて頂く立場にありません。	I am sorry but I am not in a position to answer your question.
14	ご期待に添えず申し訳ありませんでした。	We apologize for not being able to meet your expectation.
15	申し訳ありませんがそのご要望には添えません。その件については横山さんにお聞きした方がいいかと思います。	I am afraid but I cannot comply with your request. I guess you should ask Yokoyama-san about it.
16	混乱させてしまい申し訳ありません。	I am sorry for making you confused.
17	先ほどの電話会議に遅刻してしまい，大変申し訳ありません。	I apologize for being late to the conference call earlier.

4 知っていると便利なフレーズ

18	変更点をお知らせしなかったのは私どもの責任です。	It is our fault that we failed to notify you about the change.
19	ご心配をお掛けし，お詫び申し上げます。	I'm sorry for the concern／worry that I caused you.
20	今回のことであなたにご迷惑が掛からないことを願っております。	I hope this will not cause you any inconvenience.
21	本社経理部を代表して謝罪致します。	I would like to express my apology on behalf of the headquarters accounting department.

❺ クレームを言うとき

	日本語	英 語
1	提出資料が間違っています。	The document you submitted is not what I asked for.
2	ご依頼内容の意味がよく分かりません。	I do not understand your request(s).
3	質問の意図を理解されていないようですが?	Do you understand why I am asking this?
4	次回からもう少し気をつけて頂けますか?	Would you be a little more careful next time?
5	ご質問させて頂いている件についてご連絡差し上げております。	I am following up regarding the question that I asked you.
6	月次決算でなぜその資料が必要なのでしょうか?	Why do you need this document for monthly closing?
7	何故その質問に回答しなければならないのか理解できません。	I am not sure why we have to answer this question.
8	これ以上期限を延ばすのは難しいです。	It is difficult to extend the deadline further.
9	これ以上の遅延を認めるのは難しいです。	It is very difficult to allow further delay.
10	提出期限の2月10日は現実的ではありません。2月15日まで待ってもらえませんか。	The deadline of February 10 does not sound realistic. Can you wait until February 15?
11	やむを得ない事情がない限り,弁解は認められません。	I cannot accept any excuses unless there is a reasonable explanation.
12	言いたくありませんが,彼から私が送ったメールに返信頂けていないようです。	I hate to say this but I believe he has not responded to my emails.
13	あれ以来連絡がありませんが,あなたの状況をお知らせ下さい。	We have not heard from you since then. Please update your status.

14	重要な取引が私たちに報告されていませんでした。同じことが起こることは許されません。	Please be noted that there was a significant transaction that was not reported to us. We cannot afford to let this happen again.
15	期限通りに書類をご用意頂けなかった理由と，次回は期限を守って頂けるかどうか教えて頂けますか？	Please explain why you could not prepare the document on time and whether you will be able to meet our deadline next time.
16	何度も同じ質問をされているのですが，私に聞く前にそちらのチームで一度共有して頂けませんか。	I have been asked the same questions several times so far. You should better double check with your team before asking me.
17	明らかに私達はうまく連携が取れていませんね。	Clearly we do not communicate well.
18	失礼ですが，あなたの態度に私は非常に気分を害しています。	Your attitude offends me.
19	あなたは入力数値を勝手に変更するべきではありませんでした。	You are not supposed to change the numbers without approval.
20	提出された資料が何度も修正されるのは非効率的です。	Frequent amendments on the submitted documents create inefficiency.
21	彼女のファイルに入力ミスがありましたので，彼女に提出する前に内容を確認するよう伝えてもらえますか？	Could you tell her to do the self-review before submitting the file as there were a few input errors?
22	あなたの書類にいくつか誤字脱字がありました。提出前に内容を確認して下さい。	I noted a couple of typos in your document. You may want to check it before submitting it.
23	作成した資料を提出する前に一度見直し頂ければ，誤字や計算間違いなどの簡単なミスを見つけることができると思います。	You may want to double check before you submit your work so that you can catch simple mistakes such as typos or mathematical errors.

❻ 注意を促すとき

	日本語	英　語
1	弊社には鈴木は2名おります。鈴木太郎と鈴木次郎のどちらにお送り頂いたかわかりますか？	We have two Suzuki. Do you know whom you have sent it to, Taro Suzuki or Jiro Suzuki?
2	鈴木次郎は人事部のものです。経理部の鈴木太郎に再送をお願い致します。	Jiro Suzuki is in the human resources department. Please send it to Taro Suzuki of the accounting department.
3	期日の変更について交渉の余地はありません。	There is no room for negotiation of the due date.
4	昨年シートAに誤りがあり，対応に時間がかかりましたので今回はご注意下さい。	I remember that there was an error in the sheet A which took us time to deal with last year. Please be careful.
5	これ以上の入力ミスがないようご注意下さい。	Please be careful not to make any more input errors.
6	各パッケージにより金額の入力単位が異なりますのでご留意下さい。	Please note a monetary unit used for each package is different.
7	シートAのフォーマットを若干変更していますのでご注意下さい。	Please make sure that we have made minor changes to the format of sheet A.
8	昨年のファイルにシートAA，ABを追加しましたのでご注意下さい。	Please make sure that we have added the sheets AA and AB to the file we used last year.
9	シートADの計算は非常に複雑ですので特に注意して入力して下さい。	Please give special attention to the calculation in the sheet AD as it is highly complex.
10	2月6日から10日まで海外出張のため連絡できませんのでご了承下さい。	Please be informed that I will be out of the office and I will not be able to respond to you from February 6 through 10 due to an overseas business trip .
11	ご連絡有難うございます。残念ながら担当者が海外出張に行っているので，最終的な回答が遅くなってしまいそうです。	Thank you for contacting us. Unfortunately, the personnel in-charge are on a business trip abroad. Therefore, the final response will be delayed.

12	恐れ入りますが，田中は出張で不在にしております。帰社は8月29日になります。	Unfortunately, Tanaka-san is away on a business trip. He will be back on August 29.
13	予定より遅れをとっていますので，できるだけ早く手配して頂けますか？	Can you arrange it as soon as possible as it is behind schedule?
14	12/28から1/4は年末年始でお休みとなりますので，予めご承知おき下さい。	Please be informed that we will observe the New Year holidays from December 28 till January 4.

❼ 期限・督促に関係する表現

日本語	英　語
督促依頼	
1	お返事をお待ちしております。	I look forward to your reply.
2	ご返信は早ければ早いほど有難いです。	A prompt response would be very appreciated.
3	都合がつき次第お返事下さい。	Please reply at your earliest convenience.
4	日本時間の明日の17時までにご返信頂けますようお願い致します。	Please reply by 17:00 (JST) tomorrow.
5	日程がタイトですがご理解頂きたく存じます。	I know it is a tight schedule and thank you for your understanding in advance.
6	日本時間で本日中に依頼した書類を私までご提出下さい。	Please submit the documents that we requested by the end of today (JST).
7	可能であれば，明日の業務時間内にお電話頂けますでしょうか。	Could you give me a call during our office hours tomorrow?
8	今週中にご意見をお聞かせ頂きたく存じます。	Please give us your feedback by the end of this week.
9	大変な状況は存じておりますが，遅くとも来週金曜日までにご回答をお願い致します。	I understand you are busy, but I would appreciate it if you could respond by Friday next week.
10	今月末までにUSD5,000の電信送金をお願い致します。	Please remit USD5,000 by electronic transfer by the end of this month.
11	回答期限は厳守頂けますようお願い致します。	Please respond to us by the deadline.
12	期限を1日早めさせて頂けますでしょうか。	Could I make the deadline a little earlier, say one day?
13	期限内の報告が難しい場合は事前にご相談下さい。	Please let us know in advance if it is difficult to submit the document in time.
14	期日まで時間がありませんので，質問があれば，躊躇せずいつでも質問して下さい。	Please do not hesitate to contact me if you have any questions as the deadline is coming up.

	受け手側の連絡	
15	期限ぎりぎりの提出となり，大変申し訳ありません。	I am sorry for submitting the document at the last minute.
16	ご指定の期限に間に合いそうにありません。	I am afraid I will not be able to meet the deadline.
17	3月5日まで期限の延長は可能でしょうか。	Is it possible to extend the deadline to March 5?
18	日本時間の明日の朝までに提出致します。	We will submit it by tomorrow morning Japanese time.
	期日過ぎの督促・連絡	
19	提出期日を過ぎていますので，至急報告書をご提出下さい。	Please submit the report as soon as possible since it is past due.
20	回答期限は先週の金曜日でしたが，まだご回答頂けておりません。	The response was due on Friday last week, but we have not received your response yet.
21	月末から5日後にはシステム上での入力が出来なくなりますので，ご注意下さい。	Please note that the System will not accept your input subsequent to the 5th day from the month-end.
22	月末から5日経過後の連結パッケージの修正は本社で行いますので，メールでご連絡下さい。	The adjustments on the consolidation package after 5th day from the month-end will be done at the headquarters. Please notify them by email if there are adjustments to be made.

❽ 添付ファイル・メールに関係する表現

	日本語	英　語
添付ファイルの送付等		
1	添付ファイルをご参照下さい。	Please refer to the attached file.
2	取締役会議事録を添付致しました。	Please find the board of directors meeting minutes attached.
3	ご依頼のファイルを添付致します。	I have attached the file you requested.
4	先ほどのメールにはファイルが添付されていませんでした。	The file was not attached to your previous email.
5	添付ファイルを添付し忘れましたので，再送致します。	I forgot to attach the file. I am sending a new email with it attached.
6	添付ファイルが違うようです。	The attached file does not seem to be the right one.
7	添付したファイルに誤りがありましたので，こちらに差し替えをお願い致します。	I have attached the wrong file to my previous email. Please replace it with the attached.
8	添付ファイルが開けません。	I could not open the attached file.
9	添付ファイルを開きましたが，壊れているようです。	I opened the attached file but it seems to be broken.
10	添付データは何に使うのでしょうか？	What is the attached data for ?
11	添付ファイルに記入してご返信下さい。	Please fill out the attached form and submit it to us.
12	添付のエクセルファイルの"A-001"シートのD列をご参照下さい。	Please refer to column D on the sheet named "A-001" in the attached file.
13	先ほど送ったファイルは昨年のものでした。こちらの正しい添付をご参照下さい。	The file that I sent a while ago is from last year. Here is the one for this year as attached.
パスワード等		
14	添付ファイルにはパスワードがかかっています。	The attached file is password-protected.
15	添付ファイルは暗号化されています。	The attached file is encrypted.

	16	添付ファイルのパスワードは別のメールでお知らせ致します。	The password for the attached file will be sent in a separate email.
	17	添付ファイルにパスワードがかかっていて開けません。	I can't open the attached file because it is password-protected.
	18	添付ファイルのパスワードを教えて頂けますか？	Could you tell me the password for the attached file?
	容　量		
	19	添付ファイルの容量が大きいため、メールを受信できない可能性があります。本日中にメールが届かなければご連絡下さい。	You might not have been able to receive the email I sent because I attached a large file. If you will not have received my email by the end of today, please let me know.
	20	添付ファイルの容量が大きいため、メールを受信できませんでした。ファイルを分割してお送り頂けますか？	I could not receive the email due to the file size. Could you split it into several smaller files and send them to me?
	21	メールでファイルをお送りしたいのですが、メールサーバーの受信サイズ制限はありますか？	I would like to send you a file. Does your email server have any file size limitation?
	22	当社のメールサーバーは10MBまでしか受信できません。	Our email server does not accept any files over 10 megabytes.
	メール送付		
	23	長期借入金の明細表をメールでお送り頂けますか？	Could you send us the list of long-term debt by email?
	24	12月9日にお送りしたメールをご参照下さい。	Please refer to the email I sent you on December 9.
	25	当年度の決算スケジュールは先日メールでお知らせしたとおりです。	We have informed you of the current year closing schedule by email the other day.
	26	添付ファイルをご確認のうえ、折り返しメール下さい。	Please let us know by responding to this email once you go through the attached file.
	27	先ほど（2通目）のメールはご放念下さい。	Please disregard my previous (second) email.

28	メールの宛先を間違えてしまいました。先ほど私がお送りしたメールは無視して頂けますでしょうか？	Please accept my apologies for sending the wrong email to you. It would be greatly appreciated if you could disregard the email.
29	ご返信頂く際には，弊社財務部の加藤（Kato@finance.com）をCCに入れて下さい。	Please copy Mr. Kato at our finance department (Kato@finance.com) when you reply to us.
30	CCに入っている弊社財務部の斉藤宛にご返信頂けますでしょうか。	Please reply to Mr. Saito at our finance department whose email address is included in the CC field of this email.
31	どういう訳か，メールが文字化けしていて，読めません。なぜかわかりますか？	Somewhat I cannot read your message as funny characters are showing up in your message. Do you have any idea why?

❾ 定型的な言い回し

	日本語	英語
1	<u>ちなみに,</u> 本社ビルは日比谷に移転するらしいですよ。	<u>By the way,</u> the head office building may move to Hibiya next year.
2	<u>正直に言うと,</u> 私は会計のことがあまりよくわかりません。	<u>To tell you the truth,</u> I do not understand much about accounting.
3	本社営業時間は9時から17時ですので<u>ご留意下さい。</u>	<u>Please note that</u> the business hours at the headquarters are from 9am to 5pm.
4	素晴らしいご提案を有難うございます。<u>しかし,</u> ABC社の本山さんはこのプロジェクトに反対するかもしれません。	Thank you for your nice presentation. <u>However,</u> Mr. Motoyama of ABC company may be against this project.
5	わが社の業績は堅調推移しています。<u>したがって,</u> 採用人数は増加する見込みです。	Our business continues to grow. <u>Therefore,</u> the number of new hires may increase.
6	<u>また,</u> この論点についても明日までに整理する必要があります。	<u>Also,</u> we have to sort out this issue by tomorrow.
7	<u>加えて,</u> コンプレッサー事業を強化します。	<u>In addition,</u> we plan to strengthen our compressor business.
8	<u>さらに,</u> 取引価格の件についてもディスカッションする予定です。	<u>Moreover,</u> we will also discuss the transaction prices.
9	明日は祝日<u>なので,</u> 来週状況を確認しましょう。	<u>Since</u> tomorrow is a holiday, shall we confirm the status next week?
10	こみ入った話<u>なので,</u> 会議室で話しましょう。	<u>As</u> this is a complicated matter, let's talk about it in a meeting room.
11	まずIDとパスワードを入力し, <u>そして,</u>下にある「Continue」ボタンをクリックします。	Please input your user ID and password, <u>then</u> click the "Continue" button below.
12	予算達成<u>を条件に,</u> 年末賞与を大幅にアップします。	We will drastically increase the year-end bonus <u>provided that</u> we achieve the budget.
13	アジア圏での売上は増加していますが, <u>その一方で,</u> ヨーロッパでの売上は低迷しています。	Sales in the Asian countries increased. <u>On the other hand,</u> sales in Europe remained stagnant.

14	<u>一般的には，</u>人事評価は３月に行われます。	<u>In general,</u> performance evaluation is performed in March.
15	<u>厳密には，</u>あなたの指摘は正しくありません。	<u>Precisely,</u> what you have pointed out is not correct.
16	<u>言い換えると，</u>この２つは同時期に提出してもらうことになります。	<u>In other words,</u> we request you submit these two materials at the same time.
17	<u>端的にいうと，</u>以下の点が良く理解できません。	<u>In short,</u> I cannot understand the following points.
18	<u>逆にいうと，</u>その責任はあなたが負わなければならないのです。	<u>To put it another way,</u> you are responsible for the matter.
19	今日中に会議のアレンジをして下さい。<u>なぜなら，</u>資料の提出期限が今週末だからです。	Please make an arrangement of the conference by the end of today <u>because</u> we have to submit the documents by the end of this week.
20	彼女は会計だけでなく，金融についても精通しています。	She is familiar <u>not only</u> with accounting <u>but also</u> finance.
21	<u>すでにご存知かもしれませんが，</u>越智さんは定年退職されました。	<u>As you may already know,</u> Ochi-san already retired.
22	<u>すなわち</u>今月中に仕事を終わらせる必要があるということです。	<u>That is,</u> we have to finish our work by the end of this month.
23	<u>私が知る限りでは，</u>この件は監査人に伝達済みです。	<u>As far as I know,</u> this matter has been reported to the auditor.
24	身分を証明するものが<u>なければ，</u>本社ビルには入れません。	You cannot enter the headquarters building <u>unless</u> you have some kind of identification.
25	わが社は今後ビジネスモデルを大幅に変えていく予定です。<u>たとえば，</u>企業買収により医薬品事業を開拓します。	We plan to change our business model significantly. <u>For example,</u> we will start pharmaceutical businesses by M&A.
26	<u>念のため確認ですが，</u>明日は取引先のオフィスに直接向かえばいいのですよね。	<u>Just to clarify,</u> I need to go to our client's ／customer's office directly, right?

4 知っていると便利なフレーズ

27	毎度のことで恐縮ですが、承認済み支払伝票のご提出をお願いします。	<u>As it is requested every time,</u> we would like you to send us the approved disbursement slips.
28	何度も催促して申し訳ありませんが、できるだけ早く取締役会議事録をご送付下さい。	<u>Sorry for bothering you many times</u> but please send the board of directors meeting minutes to me as soon as possible.
29	つきましては、出欠をお知らせ下さいますようお願い致します。	<u>Therefore,</u> please confirm your attendance.
30	従来同様、資料の提出は経理部の田村さんにお願いします。	Please submit the related documents to Tamura-san in the accounting department <u>as usual</u>.
31	おそらくですが、先方はこの件について強く懸念を示しています。	The other party is <u>probably (perhaps)</u> concerned about this matter.
32	監査人がその会計処理に合意している限り問題ありません。	<u>As long as</u> the auditors agree with the accounting treatment, there is no problem.
33	そういった事情であれば、期限の延長は認められます。	<u>In that case,</u> extending deadlines is allowed.
34	ご参考までに、前年度のデータをお送りします。	We will send the previous year's data <u>for your reference</u>.
35	可能な限り、今日の9時までにご回答をお願い致します。	Please respond by 9pm today <u>if possible</u>.
36	昨年の状況に鑑みると、今年はもう少し提出期限を早めた方がよいでしょう。	<u>Considering</u> the situation last year, we should set a due date earlier for this year.
37	昨日のご回答に関連して、追加の質問があります。	<u>In connection with</u> your answer yesterday, we have an additional question.
38	仮にA社と取引内容の変更があったとしても、引き続きA社から製品を購入します。	<u>Even if</u> there is a change to the transaction conditions with company A, we will purchase the products from that company.

39	期限通りに回答できる<u>か，正直わか</u><u>りません</u>。	<u>I'm not sure if</u> I can respond to you in time.
40	<u>少し変な質問かもしれませんが，</u>この添付資料は本当に必要ですか。	<u>This may be strange to ask,</u> but do you really need the attached documents?
41	<u>以前同じ質問をしたかもしれません</u><u>が，</u>これは本部長が承認済みのデータでしょうか。	<u>I might have already asked you the same</u> <u>question but</u> is this data approved by the general manager?
42	<u>後学のため，</u>繰延税金資産の回収可能性の考え方についてご教授頂けますでしょうか。	<u>This is just for my knowledge.</u> Could you walk us through a basic concept of recoverability of deferred tax assets?
43	<u>お役に立つかもしれないと思ったの</u><u>で，</u>プレスリリースのリンクも下に入れておきました。	<u>In case it may be of any help,</u> I have included the link to the press release below.

4 知っていると便利なフレーズ

❿ その他の便利なフレーズ

	日本語	英語
1	了解です。 (簡易な表現／丁寧なメールでは使用しない)	Noted.
2	わかりました。 (簡易な表現／丁寧なメールでは使用しない)	Understood.
3	これは非常に助かります。	It helps me a lot.
4	お役に立てば幸いです。	I hope this would be of help to you.
5	これで回答になっているとよいのですが。	I hope this would answer your question.
6	現時点においては，進捗は50％といったところです。	The progress is (rate would be) around 50% as of now.
7	その件については現在確認中です。	Regarding this matter, we are confirming it right now.
8	誤解を避けるため，必ずCCに上長を入れるようにして下さい。	Please make sure to CC your supervisor to avoid any misunderstanding.
9	私はその回答には納得できません。	I'm not convinced with the answer.
10	この点ではあなたと意見が合致します。	I agree with you on this point.
11	指示書の内容について明確にしたいのですが，どなたにご質問すればよいでしょうか。	Who should I ask for further clarification of the instructions?
12	簡単な質問があります。	I have a quick question.
13	1点追加でお願いしてもよろしいでしょうか？	Could I add another request?
14	ひとまずドラフトだけでも送って頂けると助かります。	It would be great if you could send the draft version for now.
15	私が言いたかったのはそういうことではありません。	This is not what I meant to say.
16	もしご存知でしたら教えて頂きたいのですが，経理部はどちらにあるのでしょうか？	It would be appreciated if you could tell me where the accounting department is.

英語にはない日本語表現

 我々が日本語でよく使う表現でも英語には同じようなものがないことがあり，英語のメールを書く際に日本語と同じ感覚で書くことが困難なケースがよくあります。

 英語にはない日本語の表現の代表的な例としては以下のようなものが挙げられます。このような日本語表現については，文化的な違いとして割り切って記載しないか，または別の近い意味の言い回しにするか工夫する必要があります。

(例)

お世話になっています。
お疲れ様です。
よろしくお願いします。
いただきます。
ごちそうさま。
失礼します。
お邪魔します。
いってらっしゃい。
ご苦労様です。
遠慮します。
弊社，伺う，拝見する，承知する，などの謙譲語
御社，貴社，いらっしゃる，ご覧になる，などの尊敬語

Chapter Ⅲ
基本となる言い回しの「型」

ChapterⅢでは，経理業務で頻繁に使う定型的な言い回しをまとめました。この言い回しを押さえておけば，単語を入れ替えることにより，さまざまな場面で英文を作成することができる，怖いものなしの48パータンです。

経理業務では担当している業務が何であれ，方針を伝えたり，内容を問い合わせたり，作業を依頼したりするなどのコミュニケーションが必要な場面が多く存在します。このChapterではこういった場面でよく使う表現をまとめました。

	日本語	英　語
1	〜についてご連絡します。	
	支払処理プロセスの変更について連絡します。	We are <u>informing you of</u> several expected changes to the payment process.
2	〜へご連絡下さい。	
	質問がありましたら私へご連絡下さい。	If you have any questions, <u>please contact</u> me.
3	〜までに連絡下さい。	
	今月末までに返信下さい。	<u>Please get back to me by</u> the end of this month.
4	〜について質問があります。	
	賞与引当金の算定について質問があります。	<u>I have a question about</u> the calculation of the bonus provision.
5	〜についてご確認願います。	
	提出前に資料間の整合性を一通りご確認願います。	Before submission, <u>please make sure of</u> the consistency between documents.
6	〜という理解でよろしいでしょうか？	
	購買に関する仕訳は経理部が入力しているという理解でよろしいでしょうか？	<u>Is my understanding corret</u> that the accounting department enters purchase journal entries?
7	〜はどういう意味ですか？	
	法律上の制限とはどういう意味ですか？	<u>What do you mean by</u> the legal restrictions?
8	〜は完了していますか？	
	8月分の送金は完了していますか？	<u>Has</u> the remittance for August <u>been completed</u>?
9	どちらを〜でしょうか？	
	どちらの添付ファイルを先に見ればよいかご教示頂けますでしょうか。	<u>Do you mind if you could tell me which</u> attached files we need to see first?

10	誰に〜でしょうか？	
	顧客Aからの請求書は誰に送付されたのでしょうか。	<u>Could you tell me to whom</u> you sent the invoice from the customer A?
11	どこを〜でしょうか？	
	昨日どのシートを更新したか教えて頂けますか？	<u>Could you guide us which</u> sheets you changed yesterday?
12	何を〜でしょうか？	
	ストックオプション費用の計算に際し，何の割引率を参照したか教えて下さい。	<u>Could you tell us what</u> discount rate you referred to in calculating the share-based compensation?
13	〜を予定しています。	
	我々のレビュー完了は月曜までを予定しています。	We <u>plan to</u> complete our review by Monday.
14	〜について変更があります。	
	昨日お送りした経理担当者一覧について変更があります。	<u>There are some changes in</u> the list of accounting personnel I sent through yesterday.
15	〜に決定しました。	
	収益認識基準を出荷基準から検収基準へ変更することに決定しました。	We <u>determined to</u> change our revenue recognition policy from delivery basis to customers' acceptance basis.
16	〜が利用可能になります。	
	このチェックリストは来期から利用可能となります。	This checklist will <u>be available</u> next year.
17	〜に伝えて下さい。	
	私のコメントをTomさんに伝えて下さい。	Please <u>deliver</u> my comments to Tom-san.
18	〜を全員で共有して下さい。	
	本日の電話会議で言及した我々の懸念事項をチーム全員に共有して下さい。	Please <u>share</u> the concerns we mentioned in today's teleconference with all of your team.

19	～を周知徹底して下さい。	
	我々の検出事項を周知徹底して下さい。	Please be sure to <u>keep everyone informed</u> of our findings.
20	～を作成して下さい。	
	来年の予算を作成して下さい。	Please <u>prepare</u> the budget for the next year.
21	～を送付して下さい。	
	契約書のコピーを送付して下さい。	Please <u>send</u> me a copy of the contract.
22	～の資料を提出して下さい。	
	前回のミーティングで話した通り，修正後の受注見込を提出して下さい。	As discussed in the previous meeting, <u>please submit</u> the revised sales order forecast document.
23	～を添付して下さい。	
	見積貸借対照表，損益計算書を添付して下さい。	Please <u>attach</u> the forecasted B/S and P/L.
24	～を修正して下さい。	
	請求書日付が誤っています。修正をお願いします。	The invoice date looks wrong. <u>Please correct</u> it.
25	～に入力して下さい。	
	必要な情報を受注管理システムに入力して下さい。	<u>Please enter</u> the necessary information in the sales order monitoring system.
26	～を入手して下さい。	
	見積書を入手して下さい。	Please <u>obtain</u> a quotation.
27	～を回覧して下さい。	
	請求書については経理部へ回付し，レビューしてもらって下さい。	Please <u>circulate</u> invoices to the accounting department for their review.
28	～の承認を，～（人）にもらって下さい。	
	固定資産購入の承認は申請部門のGMにもらって下さい。	In purchasing fixed assets, <u>please obtain approval from</u> a GM who is responsible for the request.
29	～の署名・承認印がありません。	
	請求書に上長の署名・承認印がありません。	<u>There is no approval signature／seal</u> by the supervisor on the invoice

30	〜について説明して下さい。	
	今回の方針変更の詳細について説明して下さい。	Please explain the policy change in detail.
31	〜の理由を教えて下さい。	
	繰延税金資産がBSに計上されていない理由を教えて下さい。	Please tell me the reason for no deferred tax assets is shown on the B/S.
32	〜（数値）の内訳を教えて下さい。	
	当月の顧客Aに関する製品別売上高の内訳を教えて下さい。	Please tell me the breakdown of customer A's sales by product type recorded during this month.
33	〜の見解を教えて下さい。	
	引当金を計上しないという結論についての現地会計士の見解を教えて下さい。	Please tell me your auditor's view regarding your conclusion that no provision is necessary.
34	〜の所要時間を教えて下さい。	
	修正予算の策定にどれだけ時間が必要か教えて下さい。	Please tell us how much longer you need to prepare the revised budget.
35	〜の頻度を教えて下さい。	
	毎年，購買プロセスの更新をどの程度の頻度で行っているか教えて下さい。	Could you tell me how often you update the purchase process every year?
36	〜に従って下さい。	
	会計処理についてはグループ会計マニュアルに従って下さい。	Please follow our group accounting manual for the appropriate accounting treatment.
37	〜（期限）を遵守して下さい。	
	売上に関する証憑の提出期限の遵守をお願いします。	Please meet the deadline in submitting evidence relating to sales.
38	〜（提出物等）の期限が過ぎています。	
	レポーティングパッケージの提出期限が過ぎています。	The deadline for submission of the reporting package is past due.
39	〜（マニュアル・データ等）をご参照下さい。	
	グループ会計ポリシーの35ページ，セクション4をご参照下さい。	Please refer to section 4 in our group accounting policy.

40	～のフォローアップをお願いします。	
	未確認事項のフォローアップをお願いします。	<u>Please follow up on</u> all outstanding matters.
41	～について状況の報告をお願いします。	
	人件費の内訳資料の作成について、状況の報告をお願いします。	<u>Please update us on</u> the preparation of the breakdown of HR costs.
42	対応して下さい。	
	至急対応して下さい。	<u>Please take care of it</u> immediately.
43	～（の資料）が足りません。	
	請求書番号1007の請求書をまだ受け取っていません。	<u>I don't believe I've received</u> the invoice #1007.
44	～（計算シート等）にエラーがあります。	
	提出して頂いた計算シートのセルA3の式が間違っているように思います。	It appears that the formula in cell A3 in the spread sheet you submitted to us <u>is not correct</u>.
45	～と～が一致しません。	
	補助簿と総勘定元帳が一致していません。	The sub ledger <u>and</u> general ledger <u>do not reconcile to each other</u>.
46	～と～が整合しません。	
	前回提出頂いた資料と今回説明頂いた内容は整合していません。	Your explanation <u>is not consistent with</u> the information in the file you provided to us earlier.
47	～について乖離があります。	
	6月に支給された賞与が3月末の引当金額と乖離しています。	The actual bonuses paid in June <u>were different from</u> the amount accrued in March.
48	～の計上区分を教えて下さい。	
	BS上の計上区分を教えて下さい。	Please tell us <u>how you classified it</u> in the balance sheet.

メールが長すぎない？
ポイントを押さえたメールの記載

　いざ英文メールを書いてみると，数行の中に大量の情報が入ってしまい，何を言いたいかが相手に伝わらなくなってしまうことはありませんか？

　日本語のメールでは論点をはっきり伝えられるのに，英語になると言いたいことが伝えられない，相手にこちらの意図が伝わっているか不安……。そのような場合，以下の点を意識してメールを作成することで，相手に伝わりやすい記載になります。

1．論点を整理して，段落を明確に分ける

　たとえば，「Firstly」「Secondly」「Finally」といった副詞を使用し，論点や話題ごとに文章を区切ることや，「1.As for …」「2.Question about…」として，それぞれのトピックを明示し，段落を分ける。

2．ポイントや留意点を説明する際には，定型文を使って強調する

　たとえば，「What I want to say is…」「My point is…」「Please note that…」といった定型文を使い，言いたいことや留意点を明示する。

3．「いつまでに」を明確に記載する

　たとえば，「immediately」「by Friday」「by JST 17:00PM」「by April 1. at latest」「no later than 17:00 your time」など。

Chapter Ⅳ
場面別　メール表現

　一括りで「経理で使う」といっても，財務周りの業務の比重が多い人もいれば決算業務の比重が多い人もいます。主たる業務内容が違えば具体的なコミュニケーションの内容も変わってきます。
　このChapterでは電子メールでコミュニケーションすることが多いやり取りを，「連絡・依頼・回答」「質問・回答」および「クレーム・対応」という3つのパターンに区分し，それぞれを大セクションとしました。
　各大セクションでは，売上，購買，入出金，人件費（その他），予算，決算および内部統制の7つのサブセクションごとに基本となる例文を掲載し，同じ表現を言い換えた例文や，時制を変えたもの，ChapterⅡの表現を組み合わせたもの等，少し応用編の例文も用意しました。

1 子会社，取引先等への連絡・依頼・回答

　日本の親会社担当者として，本社での決定事項・確認事項・伝達事項を海外子会社担当者や海外の取引先とやり取りするという局面で，どのような表現を使ったらいいのか，実際の例文を見てみましょう。

1 売上に関する連絡・依頼・回答

Case 1　第1四半期の売上高を報告してもらう

基本文

	日本語	英　語
1	第1四半期の<u>売上高</u>を報告して下さい。	Please report the first-quarter <u>sales figures</u>.

販売予測（sales forecast）　　　製品別売上（sales by product）
受注残（order backlog）　　　　営業セグメント別売上（sales by operating segment）
売上総利益率（GP ratio）　　　粗利益／売上総利益（gross profit）
役務収益（service revenue）

展開文

	日本語	英　語
1.1	第1四半期の売上高を教えて欲しいのですが。	I would like to know the first-quarter sales figures.
1.2	第1四半期の顧客Aに対する売上高の内訳を報告して下さい。	Could you please report the breakdown of customer A's sales recorded during the first quarter?
1.3	第1四半期の売上高の報告は7月10日までに行います。	I will report the first-quarter sales figures by July 10.
1.4	売上高について2015年度第1四半期と前年同期比較を報告して下さい。	Please report the comparison between the sales of the first quarter 2015 and 2014.
1.5	第1四半期におけるセグメント別の売上高を報告して下さい。	Please report the sales amount by each segment in the first quarter.

Case 2　契約書のコピーを送付してもらう

基本文

	日本語	英　語
2	<u>契約書</u>のコピーをメールで送付して頂けますか？	**Is it possible for you to send me a copy of the <u>contract</u> by email?**

請求書（invoice）
注文書（sales order）
見積書（sales quote）
受領報告書（customer's acceptance report）
出荷報告書（shipping report）
確認状（confirmation）
基本請負契約書（Master Services Agreement）
暫定契約書（tentative contract）
ファイナンス・リース契約書（finance lease contract）
事業譲渡契約書（contract of the transfer of operation）

展開文

	日本語	英　語
2.1	契約書のコピーをクーリエで送付して頂けますか？	Is it possible for you to send me a copy of the contract by courier?
2.2	契約書のコピーをPDFファイルで、123@abc.com宛に送付して下さい。	Please email a copy of the contract in PDF format to 123@abc.com.
2.3	契約書のコピーにつきましては10月1日付けのメールで送付しております。	I sent you the copy of the contract by email on October 1.
2.4	契約書のコピーをできるだけ早くメールして下さい。	Could you send a copy of the contract by email as soon as possible?
2.5	契約書のコピーを法務部の佐藤宛にメールで送付して下さい。	Please send a copy of the contract to Mr. Sato of the legal department by email.

Case 3　取引先の決済条件について確認してもらう

基本文

	日本語	英　語
3	A社の<u>決済条件</u>を確認して下さい。	Could you please confirm A's <u>payment terms</u>?

注文（order）
注文数量（order quantity）
与信限度額（credit limit）
指定銀行（designated bank）
配送先住所（delivery address）
取引条件（term of business）
修正された決済条件（revised payment terms）
財務状態（financial position）
個別財務諸表（stand-alone financial statements）
資本金（share capital）
総資産（total assets）
利益剰余金（retained earning）
資本剰余金（additional paid-in capital）

展開文

	日本語	英　語
3.1	A社の決済条件を見直して下さい。	Could you please review A's payment terms?
3.2	A社の決済条件について確認が必要です。	We need to confirm A's payment terms.
3.3	A社の決済条件が最新のものかどうか確認して下さい。	Could you please confirm if A's payment terms are up-to-date?
3.4	取引を開始する前に，A社の決済条件を確認して下さい。	Could you please confirm A's payment terms before you start the transaction?
3.5	明日までに，A社の決済条件を確認して下さい。	Could you please confirm A's payment terms by tomorrow?

Case 4　販売実績を販売システムへ登録してもらう

基本文

	日本語	英　語
4	販売システムへ<u>販売実績</u>を登録して下さい。	Please input the <u>sales performance</u> into the sales system.

単価（unit price）
数量（quantity）
参照ID（reference ID）
取引日（transaction date）
サービス内容（nature of service）
契約期間（contract term）
為替レート（foreign currency rate）

展開文

	日本語	英　語
4.1	販売システムへ受注情報を登録して下さい。	Please input the order information into the sales system.
4.2	販売システムへ出荷数を入力して下さい。	Please input the number of shipment into the sales system.
4.3	販売システムへ最新の情報を登録して頂けますか？	Could you please input the latest information into the sales system?
4.4	販売システムへ2014年度の販売実績を商品別に登録して下さい。	Please register the 2014 sales performance into the sales system by item.
4.5	販売システムへ販売実績を登録する際には，上長の承認をもらって下さい。	Please obtain approval from your supervisor when you input the sales performance into the sales system.

Case 5　売上関連証憑の提出遅延を知らせる

基本文

	日本語	英　語
5	売上関連証憑の提出期限が過ぎています。	The <u>sales supporting document</u> is past due.

請求書（invoices）
注文書のコピー（copies of sales orders）
受領報告書（customer's acceptance reports）
返品関連証憑（evidence relating to sales return）
売上割引関連証憑（evidence relating to sales discounts）
利益計画（profit planning）
売上関連証憑（例えば，請求書）（sales supporting document（e.g. invoices））
売上関連証憑（つまり，請求書）（sales supporting document（i.e. invoices））

展開文

	日本語	英　語
5.1	売上関連証憑の提出がまだのようです。	It seems that the sales supporting document is outstanding.
5.2	売上関連証憑の提出がされていません。	I have not received the sales supporting document.
5.3	売上関連証憑の提出は昨日が締め切りでした。	The due date of the sales supporting document was yesterday.
5.4	売上関連証憑の提出期限は明日ですのでご注意下さい。	Please note that the sales supporting document will be due tomorrow.
5.5	売上関連証憑は遅くとも明日中に提出して下さい。	Please submit the sales supporting document by tomorrow at the latest.

2　購買に関する連絡・依頼・回答

Case 6　請求書を経理部へ送付してもらう

基本文

	日本語	英　語
1	<u>請求書</u>が届きましたら経理部へお送り下さい。	When you receive the <u>invoice</u>, please send it to the accounting department.

領収書（receipt）
納品書（delivery slip）
注文書（purchase order）
見積り（estimate）
購買関連証憑（documents related to purchases）
加工費の証憑（documents related to conversion cost）
開発費の明細（breakdown of development cost）

展開文

	日本語	英　語
1.1	請求書を経理部へお送り頂くことは可能でしょうか？	Is it possible to send the invoice to the accounting department?
1.2	請求書は現在どの部門で保管されているかわかりますか？　経理部に送って頂く必要があります。	Do you know which department has the invoice? It is required to be sent to the accounting department.
1.3	請求書は昨日受領致しました。すぐに経理部へ送ります。	I received the invoice yesterday. I will send it to the accounting department soon.
1.4	請求書が届きましたら社内便で経理部の佐藤までお送り下さい。	When you get the invoice, please send it to Mr. Sato of the accounting department by interoffice mail.
1.5	請求書が届きましたら財務部へコピーをお送り下さい。迅速なご対応をお願い致します。	When you get the invoice, please send a copy of it to the finance department. Your timely action will be very much appreciated.

Case 7　仕入先から相見積りを入手してもらう

基本文

	日本語	英　語
2	A社とB社から<u>相見積り</u>を入手して下さい。	Please obtain <u>competitive quotes</u> from A and B.

提案書（proposal）
製品サンプル（product sample）
デモ機（demo unit）
会社パンフレット（company brochure）
請求書ドラフト（draft invoice）

展開文

	日本語	英　語
2.1	A社とB社の両方から見積り書を入手して下さい。	Please obtain quotations from both A and B.
2.2	A社だけでなくB社からも見積り書を入手して下さい。	Please obtain quotation from B as well as A.
2.3	A社とB社から相見積りを取るべきでした。	You should have obtained competitive quotes from A and B.
2.4	原材料Gの購入に際しては，A社とB社から相見積りを取って下さい。	Please obtain competitive quotes from A and B for raw material G.
2.5	A社に決める前に，B社とC社から相見積りを取って下さい。	Please obtain competitive quotes from B and C before you choose A.

Chapter Ⅳ　場面別　メール表現

Case 8 原材料の購入実績を教えてもらう

基本文

	日本語	英 語
3	<u>原材料</u>の先月の購入額を教えて下さい。	Could you tell me the total cost of <u>raw materials</u> last month.

機械（machinery）
交換用部品（spare parts）
ソフトウェア（software）
備品（equipment）
オフィス用家具（office furniture）
保管（storage）
物流（logistic）

展開文

	日本語	英 語
3.1	原材料の先月の購入額を正確に教えて下さい。	Could you tell me the exact amount of purchase raw materials last month.
3.2	原材料の先月の購入額を私まで連絡して下さい。	Could you inform me of the total cost of raw materials last month.
3.3	原材料の先月の購入額はUSD10,000であったことをご連絡致します。	We inform you that the total cost of raw materials last month was USD10,000.
3.4	原材料の先月までの購入額を教えて下さい。	Could you tell me the accumulated cost of raw materials by the end of last month.
3.5	原材料の先月の購入額がその前月より大きく増加している要因をお教え頂けますでしょうか？	Could you tell me why the costs of raw materials last month significantly increased compared to the month before?

Case 9　購買申請書に数量誤りのあることを知らせる

基本文

	日本語	英　語
4	購買申請書の<u>数量</u>に誤りがあります。	The <u>quantity</u> in the purchase order is not correct.

日付（date）
単価（unit price）
仕入先コード（suppliers' code）
仕入先名（supplier's name）
担当者名（contact person）
減価償却期間（depreciation period）
減価償却方法（depreciation method）
取引日レート（spot rate）

展開文

	日本語	英　語
4.1	購買申請書の数量に誤りを見つけました。	We found an error in quantity in the purchase order.
4.2	購買申請書の数量が誤っていると思います。	It appears that the quantity in the purchase order is wrong.
4.3	購買申請書の数量に誤りが3か所ありました。	There were three errors in the quantity in the purchase order.
4.4	購買申請書の数量に誤りがありますので来週の月曜までに修正して下さい。	Please correct an error in the quantity in the purchase order by next Monday.
4.5	ご多忙中恐れ入りますが，購買申請書の数量に誤りがありますので修正して下さい。	Sorry to bother you but please correct an error in the quantity in the purchase order.

Case 10　購買システムと会計システムが連動していることを知らせる

基本文

	日本語	英語
5	<u>購買システム</u>と会計システムは連動しています。	The <u>purchasing system</u> and the accounting system are linked.

在庫管理システム（inventory management system）
支払システム（payment system）
単価マスタ（unit price master）
仕入先マスタ（supplier master）
原価管理システム（cost management system）
個別原価計算管理システム（job costing management system）
標準原価管理システム（standard costing management system）

展開文

	日本語	英語
5.1	購買システムのデータは会計システムに転送されます。	The data in the purchasing system is transferred to the accounting system.
5.2	購買システムと会計システムのデータは整合しています。	The data in the purchasing system and the accounting system are consistent.
5.3	来年度より購買システムは会計システムと連動する予定です。	The purchasing system and the accounting system will be linked from next year.
5.4	ご存知のことと思いますが，来年度より購買システムは会計システムと連動する予定です。	As you may know, the purchasing system and the accounting system will be linked from next year.
5.5	購買システムの入れ替えに伴い，購買システムは会計システムと連動する予定です。	As a result of the replacement of the purchasing system, the purchasing system and the accounting system will be linked.

3　入出金に関する連絡・依頼・回答

Case 11　顧客からの入金額と請求額の不一致を知らせる

基本文

	日本語	英　語
1	A社からの入金額と<u>当社の請求額</u>が不一致です。	**Cash received from customer A does not agree with <u>the amount we billed</u>.**

当社システム上のデータ（the data in our system）
当社予想金額（the amount we expected）
請求金額（invoice amount）
小切手台帳（check register）

展開文

	日本語	英　語
1.1	A社からの入金額と当社の請求額が100円だけ一致しません。	Cash received from customer A does not match with the amount we billed by JPY 100.
1.2	A社からの入金額と当社の請求額が異なっています。	Cash received from customer A differs from the amount we billed.
1.3	A社からの入金額と当社の請求額の不一致は，当月解消しました。	Inconsistency between cash received from customer A and the amount we billed was fixed this month.
1.4	A社からの入金額と当社の請求額の不一致についてフォローアップをお願いします。	Please follow up on the inconsistency between cash received from customer A and the amount we billed.
1.5	A社からの入金額と当社の請求額の不一致について理由を教えて下さい。	Please tell me the reason for the inconsistency between cash received from customer A and the amount we billed.

Case 12　送金を至急取り消してもらう

基本文

	日本語	英　語
2	<u>送金</u>を至急取り消して下さい。	**Please cancel the <u>remittance</u> immediately.**

支払い（payment）
払戻の請求（claim for refund）
国際送金（international transfer）
支払いの実行（execution of the payment）

展開文

	日本語	英　語
2.1	送金を取り消すことは可能でしょうか？	Is it possible to cancel the remittance?
2.2	至急，送金の取り消しをお願いします。	We need you to cancel the remittance immediately.
2.3	即座に送金を取り消すべきでした。	You should have canceled the remittance immediately.
2.4	送金を至急取り消して，仕入れ先に電話して下さい。	Please cancel the remittance immediately and then make a call to the supplier.
2.5	今のところ，送金の取り消しのみ対応願います。	For now, we only need you to cancel the remittance.

Case 13　代金の振込みを依頼する

基本文

	日本語	英　語
3	<u>代金</u>を弊社口座へお振込み下さい。	Please kindly transfer your <u>payment</u> into our account.

保証金（guarantee deposit）
手付金（deposit）
違約金（penalty charges）
登録手数料（registration fee）
残りの代金（remaining payment）
信用枠供与手数料（arrangement fee）
銀行手数料（bank charges）

展開文

	日本語	英　語
3.1	代金をお振込み頂いたかどうかお知らせ下さい。	Please let us know if you have transferred your payment.
3.2	代金のお振込みの処理状況のご確認をお願いします。	Please check the status of the payment by electronic transfer.
3.3	午後3時までに、代金を弊社口座へお振込み下さい。	Please kindly transfer your payment into our account by 3pm.
3.4	支払期日到来のお知らせです。代金を弊社口座へお振込み下さい。	This is a reminder of the due date. Please kindly transfer your payment into our account.
3.5	これ以上の遅延を認めることはできません。至急、代金を弊社口座へお振込み下さい。	We cannot allow further delay. Please kindly transfer your payment into our account immediately.

Case 14　入金が確認できたことを連絡する

基本文

	日本語	英　語
4	貴社からの<u>入金</u>が確認できたことを連絡致します。	Please be informed that we confirmed your <u>payment</u>.

振込み（bank transfer）
海外送金（outbound money transfer）
返金（refund）
分納1回目の支払い（first installment payment）
解約料（cancellation fee）
立替費用（reimburse for expenses）
一括払い（lump-sum payment）

展開文

	日本語	英　語
4.1	請求書番号1006に対する貴社からの入金が確認できたことを連絡します。	We inform you that your payment on the invoice #1006 has been confirmed.
4.2	先月のサービスに対する貴社からの入金が確認できたことを連絡します。	Please be informed that we confirmed your payment for our last month's service.
4.3	先ほど営業担当者より貴社からの入金が確認できた旨連絡があったことをお伝えします。	We were just informed by our sales representative that your payment has been confirmed.
4.4	貴社からのB銀行の口座への入金が確認できたことを連絡します。	We would like to inform you that we confirmed your payment to our account in bank B.
4.5	申し訳ございませんが、貴社からの入金は明日の朝まで確認できません。	We regret to inform you that we cannot confirm your payment until tomorrow morning.

Case 15　支払期日を変更してもらう

基本文

	日本語	英　語
5	<u>支払期日</u>を変更頂くことは可能でしょうか?	**Could you change the <u>due date</u> of the payment?**

決済日 (settlement date)
受取人 (payee)
支払口座 (paying account)
送金手数料の負担当事者 (party who bears remittance costs)

展開文

	日本語	英　語
5.1	支払期日を延長頂くことは可能でしょうか?	Could you extend the due date of the payment?
5.2	支払期日の延長をご再考頂けますでしょうか?	Could you consider extending the due date of the payment?
5.3	来期から支払期日を変更して頂くことは可能でしょうか?	Could you change the due date of the payment from next year?
5.4	支払期日を10月末日から11月末日へご変更頂けないでしょうか?	Could you change the payment due date from the end of October to the end of November?
5.5	支払期日の変更依頼を頂きましたが,確認のため,メールでもご連絡頂けますでしょうか?	We have just received your request to change the payment due date. Could you please also email us just in case?

4　人件費（その他）に関する連絡・依頼・回答

Case 16　新しい給与規定に基づき給与計算を行ってもらう

基本文

	日本語	英語
1	新しい規定に基づき<u>給与</u>の計算をして下さい。	Please calculate <u>payroll</u> based on the new policy.

賞与（bonus）
引当金（allowance）
減価償却費（depreciation cost）
売上原価（cost of sales）
過去勤務費用（prior service cost）
役員報酬（directors' compensation）
基本給（base salary）

展開文

	日本語	英語
1.1	給与計算に際しては最新の規定をご参照下さい。	Please refer to the new policy when you carry out your payroll processing.
1.2	給与計算に際しては最新の規定に基づき実施されていることをご確認下さい。	Please make sure that you perform the payroll calculation based on the new policy.
1.3	新しい給与規定は次の四半期より適用されます。	The new payroll policy will be in effect from next quarter.
1.4	以前お伝えした通り，新しい規定に基づき給与の計算をして頂く必要があります。	As we informed you earlier, you need to calculate payroll based on the new policy.
1.5	来年度期首より新しいグローバル給与規定に移行致します。このため貴社は新しい規定に基づき給与の計算をして頂く必要があります。	We will switch to a new global payroll policy from the beginning of next year. Accordingly, you will need to calculate payroll based on the new policy.

Case 17　賞与額算定の前提条件を教えてもらう

基本文

	日本語	英　語
2	<u>賞与額算定の前提条件</u>を教えて下さい。	Please advise us of the assumptions used in your <u>bonus</u> calculation.

給与（payroll）
時間外手当（overtime payment）
福利厚生費（welfare expense）
有給休暇引当金（vacation accrual）
退職給付債務（projected benefit obligation）
残存価額（salvage value）

展開文

	日本語	英　語
2.1	賞与額算定の前提として何が使用されているのでしょうか？	Please advise us of what assumptions you used in your bonus calculation.
2.2	賞与支給額の前提条件に関する情報が必要です。	We would like to know the assumptions you used in your bonus calculation.
2.3	賞与支給額の前提条件に関する情報が3営業日以内に必要です。	We would like to know the assumptions you used in your bonus calculation in three business days.
2.4	前期と比較し，変更した賞与支給額の前提条件があれば教えて下さい。	Please advise us of the assumptions you used in your bonus calculation which you updated from the prior year, if any.
2.5	支給実績が予算を上回ったようですが，賞与額算定の前提条件を教えて下さい。	It appears that the bonus paid during this year was greater than the budgeted amount. Please advise us the assumptions used in your bonus calculation.

Case 18　税務申告書の提出を促す

基本文

	日本語	英語
3	<u>税務申告書</u>を提出して下さい。	Please file your <u>tax return</u>.

　　修正申告書（amended tax return）
　　還付請求（claim for refund）
　　電子版のフォーム（e-file form）
　　法人税の申告期限延長申請書（application for extension of time to file corporate income tax）
　　申告書別表M-3（schedule for M-3）

展開文

	日本語	英語
3.1	税務申告書の提出はお済みでしょうか？	Have you filed your tax return?
3.2	税務申告書を税務当局に提出して下さい。	Please file your tax return with the relevant tax authority.
3.3	税務申告書の提出はタイムリーにお願いします。	Please file your tax return in a timely manner.
3.4	税務申告書を期限内に提出できなかった場合は詳細な理由が必要です。	We need a detailed explanation if you fail to file your tax return by the due date.
3.5	従来通り，税務申告書の控えをお送り頂けますでしょうか？	As always, could you send us a copy of your tax return?

Case 19 不正行為に関する社内の調査結果を教えてもらう

基本文

	日本語	英 語
4	不正行為に関する<u>社内の</u>調査結果を報告して下さい。	Could you report to us the result of the <u>internal investigation</u> regarding the fraudulent activities?

外部の調査（external investigation）
当局による調査（investigation by the authority）
法令順守に関する従業員調査（employee survey on compliance）
第三者委員会の調査（independent committee investigation）

展開文

	日本語	英 語
4.1	不正行為に関する社内の調査結果の報告が必要です。	It is necessary for you to report to us the result of the internal investigation regarding the fraudulent activities.
4.2	不正行為に関する社内の調査結果を共有して下さい。	Could you share the result of the internal investigation regarding the fraudulent activities?
4.3	不正行為に関する社内の調査結果を9月末までに報告して下さい。	Could you report to us the result of the internal investigation regarding the fraudulent activities by the end of September.
4.4	法務部と連携して社内調査を実施し，報告して下さい。	Please conduct an internal investigation together with legal department and report to us the result of the investigation.
4.5	不正行為に関する社内調査を実施します。適切に従業員への周知をお願いします。	We will conduct an in-house investigation regarding the fraudulent activities. Please keep all employees informed about the investigation as appropriate.

Case 20 顧問弁護士の見解を入手してもらう

基本文

	日本語	英　語
5	<u>顧問弁護士</u>の見解を入手して下さい。	Please obtain an opinion from <u>our legal adviser</u>.

企業内弁護士（in-house lawyer）
社外の専門家（third party specialist）
年金数理人（actuary）
税務当局（tax authority）
引受人（underwriter）
法務部（legal department）
原告の代理人（agent of plaintiff）
被告の代理人（agent of defendant）
仲裁人（arbitrator）
裁判所（court, tribunal）

展開文

	日本語	英　語
5.1	顧問弁護士の見解は入手済みでしょうか？	Did you obtain an opinion from our legal adviser?
5.2	顧問弁護士の見解は必ず入手して下さい。	It is mandatory for you to obtain an opinion from our legal adviser.
5.3	顧問弁護士の見解の入手予定日をお知らせ下さい。	Please tell us the target date you plan to obtain an opinion from our legal adviser.
5.4	顧客との間で係争が発生した場合、いつも顧問弁護士の見解を入手しています。	We usually obtain a letter from our legal adviser when a dispute arises with our customer.
5.5	弁護士の見解を入手するのには、時間がかかります。	It takes a while to obtain an opinion from our legal adviser.

5　予算に関する連絡・依頼・回答

Case 21　予算の提出を早めてもらう

基本文

	日本語	英　語
1	予算を<u>1週間早く</u>提出して頂くことは可能でしょうか？	Would it be possible for you to submit the budget to us <u>one week earlier</u>?

1日前（one day earlier）
5営業日前（5 business days earlier）
来週の金曜までに（by next Friday）
今日中に（by the end of today）
できるだけ早く（upon your earliest convenience）
このEメールを受け取ったらすぐに（upon receipt of this email）

展開文

	日本語	英　語
1.1	予算の提出期限を1週間前倒すことは可能でしょうか？	Would it be possible for you to accelerate the deadline of the budget submission by one week?
1.2	予算を1週間早く提出して頂くことは現実的でしょうか？	Would it be realistic for you to submit the budget to us one week earlier?
1.3	来期より1週間早く予算を提出して頂くことは実務的に可能でしょうか？	Will it be practically possible for you to submit the budget to us one week earlier from next year?
1.4	ひとまず予算のドラフトだけでも送って頂けると助かります。	It would be great if you could send us the draft budget for now.
1.5	急なお知らせで申し訳ありませんが、予算を1週間早く提出して頂けますか？	Sorry for the short notice, could you please submit the budget to us one week earlier?

Case 22　売上予算のセグメント別データをメールで送ってもらう

基本文

	日本語	英　語
2	<u>売上予算のセグメント別</u>の明細データを拝見したいのですが，Eメールで送って頂けますか？	We would like to confirm the breakdown of the <u>sales budget by segment</u>, so could you send it by email, please?

製品ライン別の見積原価（the estimated cost by product line）
カテゴリー別の見積一般管理費（estimated general expense by category）
支社別の見積設備投資額（estimated capital expenditure by branch）
半期予算（half year budget）
年間EBITDA予測（annual EBITDA forecast）
変動費（variable costs）
固定費（fixed costs）
資産計上したソフトウェア費用（capitalized costs of software）

展開文

	日本語	英　語
2.1	売上予算のセグメント別の明細データを添付致します。	I have attached the breakdown of the sales budget by segment.
2.2	売上予算のセグメント別の明細データを拝見したいのですが，ドラフト版で構いませんので，最新のものを送付して頂けますか？	We would like to look over the breakdown of the sales budget by segment, so could you kindly send the latest version? The draft version would be fine.
2.3	売上予算のセグメント別の明細データについて，今後はEメールで期限内に提出して下さい。	Please submit the breakdown of the sales budget by segment by email on time in the future.
2.4	売上予算のセグメント別の明細データを拝見しました。提出頂いた予算について，お話できる時間はありますか？	We reviewed the breakdown of the sales budget by segment. Do you have time to discuss the budget with us?
2.5	売上予算のセグメント別の明細データを拝見しました。提出頂いた予算についてディスカッションしたいので，電話会議をセッティングさせて下さい。	We confirmed the breakdown of the sales budget by segment. I would like to arrange a call to discuss it with you.

Case 23　予算と実績の差異について分析してもらう

基本文

	日本語	英　語
3	<u>当年度の</u>予算と実績の差異について分析を行って下さい。	Please analyze the difference between the budget and the results <u>in this fiscal year</u>.

現在までの（to date）
先月までの（until last month）
９月30日に終了する９か月間の（for nine months period ended September 30）

展開文

	日本語	英　語
3.1	当年度の予算と実績の差異について、分析した結果を報告して下さい。	Please report the results of your variance analysis of the budget and the results in this fiscal year.
3.2	予算と実績の比較および差異分析については、月次で行って下さい。	Please perform the variance analysis of the budget and the results monthly.
3.3	当年度の予算と実績の差異について、分析した結果を至急報告して下さい。	Could you report the results of your variance analysis between budget and results in this fiscal year immediately, please.
3.4	予算と実績の差異分析結果について、四半期毎に電話会議で報告して下さい。	Please report the result of an analysis for differences between budget and result every quarter at the conference call.
3.5	売上総利益の予実差異分析については、製品セグメント毎に行うようにして下さい。	Please perform the variance analysis between budget and results of the gross margin by product segment.

Case 24　予算達成率を報告してもらう

基本文

	日本語	英 語
4	<u>予</u>算達成率を報告して下さい。	Please report the achievement rate against your <u>target budget</u>.

年間目標値（annual target）
修正後目標値（revised target）
四半期予算（quarterly budget）
販売予測（sales forecast）
最新の予算（latest budget）
有利子負債（interest bearing debt）
ソルベンシーマージン率（solvency margin ratio）
目標運転資金（target working capital）
目標回転率（target turnover ratio）
目標回収可能額（target recoverable amount）

展開文

	日本語	英 語
4.1	四半期毎の予算達成率が報告されていないようです。ご確認下さい。	I believe that you have not yet reported to us the achievement rate against your target. Can you please check the status?
4.2	予算達成率の報告の担当者は誰ですか？　至急，報告書を提出して下さい。	Could you tell me who is in charge of reporting the achievement rate against your target? The report should be submitted immediately.
4.3	四半期毎に予算達成率を報告して下さい。	Please report the achievement rate against your target every quarter.
4.4	予算達成率が75%を下回った場合，その原因と今後の対策を報告して下さい。	If the achievement rate falls below 75%, please report the cause and your action plan to us.
4.5	予算達成率はマネージャーの業績評価に関係しますので，必ず報告して下さい。	Please make sure to report the achievement rate against your target because it affects manager's performance evaluation.

Case 25　来年の購買予算を作成してもらう

基本文

	日本語	英語
5	来年の<u>購買予算</u>を作成して下さい。	Please prepare the <u>purchase budget</u> for the next year.

売上予算（sales budget）
販売計画（sales plan）
会社予算（company budget）
部門予算（department budget）
広告費予算（budget for advertisement）
販促費予算（budget for promotional costs）
見積減価償却費（estimated depreciation expense）
見積償却費（estimated amortization expense）

展開文

	日本語	英語
5.1	来年の購買予算の作成にすでに取り掛かっているか教えて下さい。	Please let me know if you have already started to prepare the purchase budget for the next year.
5.2	来年の購買予算の作成はいつ頃できますでしょうか？	Could I ask you when you can prepare the purchase budget for next year?
5.3	来年の購買予算につきましては今週中には作成できると思います。	We should be able to prepare the purchase budget for the next year within this week.
5.4	来年の購買予算を今年のコスト実績と比較して作成して下さい。	Please prepare the next year's purchase budget by comparing the current year actual costs incurred.
5.5	来年の購買予算は当年度実績額の95%以内になるよう作成して下さい。	Please prepare the purchase budget for the next year which will be 95% or less than the actual costs incurred during this year.

6　決算に関する連絡・依頼・回答

Case 26　当期のパッケージ提出スケジュールを知らせる

基本文

	日本語	英　語
1	当期の<u>連結パッケージ</u>提出スケジュールは添付資料の通りです。	Please find the attached this year's reporting schedule for your <u>reporting packages</u>.

税務申告書のドラフト（draft tax return）
補足帳票（supplementary schedules）
内部取引一覧表（list of intercompany transactions）
現地GAAPベースの財務諸表（local GAAP based financial statements）
関連当事者一覧表（list of related parties）
精算表（worksheet）
解約不能リース一覧表（list of non-cancellable leases）
決算仕訳（closing entries）

展開文

	日本語	英　語
1.1	当期の連結パッケージ提出スケジュールは以下の通りです。	This year's reporting schedule for your reporting packages is as follows:
1.2	当期の連結パッケージ提出期限は4月6日です。	Your reporting package is due on April 6.
1.3	当期の連結パッケージ提出スケジュールについては別途ご連絡致します。	We will let you know later about this year's reporting schedule for your reporting packages.
1.4	当期の連結パッケージの提出期限は3日後ですので、遅れないようによろしくお願いします。	Please submit this year's reporting packages on a timely manner, since they will be due in three days.
1.5	当期の連結パッケージの提出スケジュールが延期され、提出期限が4月6日になりました。	The due date of this year's reporting packages has been postponed and will be due on April 6.

Case 27　パッケージフォームの変更を知らせる

基本文

	日本語	英　語
2	当期から<u>パッケージのフォーム</u>が変わりました。	We modified the <u>reporting package form</u> this year.

報告期限（reporting deadline）
収益認識基準（revenue recognition policy）
必要なエビデンスの種類（type of evidence required）
連絡先担当者（contact person）
棚卸資産評価損の計上要件（criteria to record a loss on devaluation of inventory）
減損の兆候を識別するためのプロセス（process to identify indication of an impairment）
原価計算基準（cost accounting policy）
加重平均資本コスト（weighted average cost of capital（WACC））

展開文

	日本語	英　語
2.1	当期からパッケージのフォームが添付のように変わりました。	As attached, we modified the reporting package form this year.
2.2	当期は既存のパッケージのフォームに変更はありません。	No modifications have been made on the existing reporting package form this year.
2.3	来期からパッケージのフォームが変わります。	We will modify the reporting package form next year.
2.4	パッケージのフォームが若干変わりましたが，前期からの大幅な変更点はありません。	Although we made minor modifications on the reporting package form, there are no significant changes compared to last year's form.
2.5	当期からパッケージのフォームが変わりましたので，新しいフォームをお送りします。	As we modified the reporting package form this year, attached is the new one for you.

Case 28 特定のフォームについて提出する必要のない旨を知らせる

基本文

	日本語	英　語
3	あなたの会社は<u>フォームA</u>を提出する必要はありません。	Your Company does not have to submit the <u>Form A</u>.

売掛金年齢表（AR aging list）
固定資産受払表（list of addition/disposal of fixed assets）
引当金明細表（breakdown of provisions）
滞留在庫のリスト（list of slow-moving inventory）
関係会社債権債務一覧表（list of intercompany receivables/payables）
遊休資産（long-lived assets temporarily idled）
取得原価で評価した資産のリスト（list of assets valued at acquisition cost）
株主のリスト（list of stockholders）
繰延税金資産の明細（breakdown of deferred tax assets）
リース資産のリスト（list of lease assets）
リース債務のリスト（list of lease obligation）
定期預金のリスト（list of term deposits）

展開文

	日本語	英　語
3.1	あなたの会社はフォームAを提出しなければなりません。	Your Company is required to submit the Form A.
3.2	あなたの会社はフォームAを提出すべきでした。	Your Company should have submitted the Form A.
3.3	あなたの会社は翌期よりフォームAの提出が不要となる見込みです。	From next year, your Company will be exempt from the submission of the Form A.
3.4	あなたの会社はフォームAを提出する必要はありません。その替わりフォームBを提出して下さい。	Your Company does not have to submit the Form A. Instead, please submit the Form B.
3.5	会計方針について変更がなければ、あなたの会社はフォームAを提出する必要はありません。	Your Company does not have to submit the Form A unless you change something on your accounting policy.

Case 29　月次決算での為替レートについて知らせる

基本文

	日本語	英　語
4	<u>月次決算での為替の適用レート一覧表</u>を送ります。	**We will send you the <u>list of foreign currencies used for the monthly closing</u>.**

四半期決算での為替の適用レート一覧表（list of foreign currencies used for the quarterly closing）

最新のグループ会計方針（latest group accounting policy）

当期決算の留意事項（key notes for this year's closing）

決算スケジュール（closing schedule）

最新のコンタクトリスト（most up-to-date contact list）

評価性引当金のためのテンプレート（template for valuation allowances）

為替差益（損）の分析（analysis of foreign currency exchange gain（loss））

税率（tax rate）

実効税率（effective tax rate）

期末日レートのリスト（list of closing rates）

展開文

	日本語	英　語
4.1	月次決算での為替の適用レートについては添付ファイルをご参照下さい。	Please refer to the attached list of foreign currencies used for the monthly closing.
4.2	月次決算での為替の適用レート一覧表は8時に送付済みです。	We already sent at 8:00am the list of foreign currencies used for the monthly closing.
4.3	月次決算での為替の適用レート一覧表は，来月の頭にお送りする予定です。	We will send you the list of foreign currencies used for the monthly closing at the beginning of next month.
4.4	先程お送りした月次決算での為替の適用レート一覧表は誤っていますので，こちらをお使い下さい。	Please use this as the list of foreign currencies for the monthly closing. The list we sent you earlier contains errors.
4.5	もし必要であれば，月次決算での為替の適用レート一覧表を送ります。	We will send you the list of foreign currencies used for the monthly closing, if necessary.

Case 30　連結システムの入力期限について知らせる

基本文

	日本語	英語
5	<u>連結システムへの入力</u>は既に締め切りました。	**<u>Entries to the consolidation system</u> have been closed already.**

経理システムへの入力（entries to the accounting system）
本社経理部への問い合わせ（questions to the accounting department）
システムでの調整仕訳入力（adjusting entries through system）
100万円未満の修正（revising entries smaller than JPY 1 million）
連結システムの操作方法に関する一般的な質問（general questions about how to operate the consolidation system）

展開文

	日本語	英語
5.1	連結システムへの入力は既に受け付けておりません。	We cannot accept any more entries to the consolidation system.
5.2	連結システムへの入力は4月10日に締め切りました。	We closed entries to the consolidation system on April 10.
5.3	連結システムへの入力は明日締め切る予定になっています。	We will close entries to the consolidation system tomorrow.
5.4	連結システムへの入力期限は4月10日までですので，ご注意下さい。	Please make sure that entries to the consolidation system must be completed by April 10.
5.5	連結システムへの入力は4月10日に締め切りましたので，今後は直接本社経理部にご連絡下さい。	Please directly contact the accounting department in the head office as we already closed entries to the consolidation system on April 10.

7 内部統制に関する連絡・依頼・回答

Case 31 売上プロセスに係るフローチャートを作成してもらう

基本文

	日本語	英　語
1	売上プロセスに係る<u>フローチャート</u>を作成して下さい。	Could you please prepare a <u>flow chart</u> of the sales process?

業務記述書（business process description）
リスク・コントロール・マトリクス（risk control matrix）
データ・フローチャート（data flow chart）
ウォークスルー資料（walk-through documents）
統制テスト文書（work papers for tests of controls）

展開文

	日本語	英　語
1.1	売上プロセスに係るフローチャートが作成されていないようです。	It seems that a flow chart of the sales process has not been prepared.
1.2	売上プロセスに係る業務記述書だけでなくフローチャートも作成して下さい。	Could you please prepare not only a process description but also a flow chart of the sales process?
1.3	売上プロセスに係るフローチャートの作成状況を教えて下さい。	Could you please update the current status of preparation of the flow chart of the sales process?
1.4	売上プロセスはJ-SOXの対象です。フローチャートを作成して下さい。	The sales process is in scope of J-SOX documentation. Please prepare a flow chart of the process.
1.5	売上プロセスに係る文書化は完了しています。	We have completed the documentation of the sales process.

Case 32 人件費プロセスに係る統制テストを実施してもらう

基本文

	日本語	英語
2	人件費プロセスに係る<u>統制テスト</u>を実施して下さい。	Could you please perform the <u>test of controls</u> for the payroll process?

ウォークスルー（walkthrough）
アップデートテスト（update testing）
IT統制のテスト（test of IT application controls）
マニュアル統制のテスト（test of manual controls）
レビュー統制のテスト（test of review controls）

展開文

	日本語	英語
2.1	前期と同様に，人件費プロセスに係る統制テストを実施して下さい。	Similar to the prior year, please perform the test of controls for the payroll process.
2.2	人件費プロセスに係る統制テストをいつ実施する予定か教えてもらえますか？	Can you tell us when you are going to perform the tests of controls for the payroll process?
2.3	人件費プロセスに係る統制テストを完了して下さい。	Please complete the tests of controls for the payroll process.
2.4	人件費プロセスに係る統制テストの結果を教えて下さい。	Please tell us the results of the tests of controls for the payroll process.
2.5	現時点では人件費プロセスに係る統制テストは10月に実施する予定です。	At this stage, we will perform the tests of controls for the payroll process in October.

Case 33 統制不備に関する要約表を送ってもらう

基本文

	日本語	英　語
3	<u>統制不備要約表</u>を送って下さい。	Please send us <u>a summary of control deficiencies</u>.

　　識別されたエラー（errors identified）
　　気付事項（your findings）
　　重要な不備（significant deficiencies）
　　重大な欠陥（material weaknesses）
　　是正措置（your remedial actions）

展開文

	日本語	英　語
3.1	統制の不備があった場合は要約表に記載して下さい。	If there are control deficiencies, please note that in the summary of control deficiencies.
3.2	統制不備要約表は提出される必要があります。	The summary of control deficiencies must be submitted to us.
3.3	提出期限までに統制不備要約表を必ず提出して下さい。	Please make sure you submit the summary of control deficiencies by the deadline.
3.4	統制不備要約表に記載された項目の改善計画を策定し，送って下さい。	Please create and send us the remediation plan for the items noted in the summary of control deficiencies.
3.5	今年は統制の不備は識別されませんでした。	We have not identified any control deficiencies this year.

Case 34　購買プロセスに係るリスクの見直しを行ってもらう

基本文

	日本語	英　語
4	購買プロセスに係る<u>リスク</u>の見直しをお願いします。	Please re-examine the <u>risks</u> of the purchase process.

　　統制（controls）
　　サブ・プロセス（sub processes）
　　プロセス・オーナー（process owner）
　　テスト戦略（testing strategy）
　　利益操作のリスク（manipulation risks）
　　架空取引のリスク（risks of fictitious transactions）

展開文

	日本語	英　語
4.1	購買プロセスに係るリスクについて，ざっと見直して下さい。	Please make a general review of the risks of the purchase process.
4.2	購買プロセスに係るリスクについて，全体的に見直して下さい。	Can you conduct an overall review of the risks of the purchase process?
4.3	購買プロセスに係るリスクの見直しはいつまでに完了する予定ですか？	Could you tell me when the revised risk assessment over the purchase process will be completed?
4.4	リスク・コントロール・マトリクスに記載されているリスクの見直しをお願いします。	It would be great if you could re-examine the risks described in the risk control matrix.
4.5	購買プロセスに係るリスクの見直しをお願いします。リスクについては，財務報告に係るリスクに限定して下さい。	Please re-assess the risks of the purchase process. The risks should be limited to those relevant to financial reporting.

Case 35 承認済みの全社統制チェックリストを送ってもらう

基本文

	日本語	英　語
5	承認済みの<u>全社統制チェックリスト</u>を送付して下さい。	**Please send us an approved <u>company level controls checklist</u>.**

財務諸表作成プロセス（financial statement closing process）
内部統制自己評価（internal controls self-assessment）
経営者評価（management assessment）
監査計画と対象範囲（audit planning and scoping）
IT全般統制（IT general controls）
持株会社のIT全般統制（IT general controls of holding company）

展開文

	日本語	英　語
5.1	全社統制チェックリストは，承認を受けてから提出して下さい。	The Company level checklist should be approved before submission.
5.2	承認済みの全社統制チェックリストを早急に提出頂けますと幸いです。	It would be appreciated if you could send us an approved Company level check list immediately.
5.3	承認済みの全社統制チェックリストが送付されるべきでした。	You should have sent us an approved Company level checklist.
5.4	承認済みの全社統制チェックリストを送付して下さい。日程がタイトですがご理解頂きたく存じます。	Please send us an approved Company level checklist. I understand it is a tight schedule and thank you for your understanding in advance.
5.5	申し訳ありませんが，本部長が出張中のため，再送には少し時間がかかります。	I'm sorry, but it will take a while to resend it because the general manager is on a business trip.

2 子会社，取引先等への質問・回答

海外子会社の担当者とメールのやり取りをする中で，詳細や不明な点等について相手に質問を投げかける場面や，相手からの質問に対して回答を行う局面が多々生じます。そのような場合にどのような表現をするのか，実際の例文で確認してみましょう。

1 売上に関する質問・回答

Case 36　請求書の発行担当者について問い合わせる

基本文

	日本語	英　語
1	貴社の<u>請求書発行</u>の担当者を教えて頂けますか？	Could you please introduce me to the person in charge of <u>issuing invoices</u>?

売上仕訳入力（inputting of sales journal entries）　出荷業務（delivery）
返品処理（sales returns）　契約締結（binding contracts）　債権回収（AR collection）

展開文

	日本語	英　語
1.1	貴社の請求書発行の担当者に変更がありましたか？	Did the person in charge of issuing invoices change?
1.2	弊社の請求書発行の担当者は田中になります。	Tanaka-san is the person in charge of issuing invoices.
1.3	貴社の請求書発行の担当者をご連絡頂いておりましたでしょうか？	Have you informed us of the person in charge of issuing invoices yet?
1.4	火曜日に届いた請求書について質問があるのですが，貴社の請求書発行の担当者を教えて頂けますか？	We have a question about the invoice that arrived last Tuesday. Could you please introduce me to the person in charge of issuing invoices?
1.5	以前同じ質問をしたかもしれませんが，貴社の請求書発行の担当者を教えて頂けますか？	I may have already asked you this question before, but could you please introduce me to the person in charge of issuing invoices?

Case 37　顧客の与信情報を確認したかどうかについて問い合わせる

基本文

	日本語	英　語
2	<u>顧客の与信情報</u>は確認しましたか？	Have you checked <u>the customer's credit information</u>?

エラーメッセージ（error messages）
見積書の内容（contents of the quotation）
契約書の付属文書（addendum to the contract）
関連する関係会社間取引（relevant inter-company transactions）
返品権（right of return）
検査結果（inspection result）

展開文

	日本語	英　語
2.1	顧客の与信情報は更新していますか？	Have you updated the customer's credit information?
2.2	残念ながら，顧客の与信情報はまだ確認していません。	Unfortunately, we have not checked the customer's credit information.
2.3	いつ顧客の与信情報を確認する予定ですか？	When will you check the customer's credit information?
2.4	与信限度額を超えた売掛金残高が計上されていますので，顧客の与信情報を確認して下さい。	You should check the customer's credit information as the customer's AR balance exceeds the credit limit.
2.5	顧客情報が販売管理システムに登録されていないようですが，顧客の与信情報は確認しましたか？	It seems the customer information is not recorded in the sales management system. Have you checked the customer's credit information?

Case 38 顧客への支払督促の頻度について問い合わせる

基本文

	日本語	英　語
3	顧客への<u>支払</u>の督促はどのくらいの頻度で実施していますか？	How often do you follow up with customers on their <u>payment</u>?

出荷（delivery）
請求書（invoice）
リベート（rebate）
未着品（undelivered goods）
先払いの手数料（up-front fee）
成果報酬（performance-based fee）

展開文

	日本語	英　語
3.1	顧客への支払の督促は毎日実施して下さい。	You should follow up with customers on their payment every day.
3.2	顧客への支払の督促はできるだけ多く実施するようにしています。	We try to follow up with customers on their payment as often as possible.
3.3	前回の顧客への支払の督促はいつ行いましたか？	When did you last follow up with the customer on their payment?
3.4	売掛金が90日以上滞留していますが，顧客への支払の督促はどのくらいの頻度で実施していますか？	The customer's AR balance is 90 days overdue. How often do you follow up with the customer on their payment?
3.5	滞留している売掛金残高が100万円を超える顧客への支払の督促はどのくらいの頻度で実施していますか？	How often do you follow up on payments with customers whose outstanding AR balance exceeds JPY 1 million?

Case 39 売上取引の根拠資料の有無について問い合わせる

基本文

	日本語	英 語
4	<u>9月の1億円を超える売上取引の根拠資料</u>はありますか？	**Can you send us <u>supporting documents for individual September sales transactions that exceeded JPY 100 million</u>?**

株式譲渡契約（Stock Purchase Agreement（SPA））
定款（a copy of Articles of Corporation）
経営会議議事録（management meeting minutes）
役務提供の根拠資料（supporting document for service rendered）

展開文

	日本語	英 語
4.1	9月の1億円を超える売上取引の根拠資料をPDFにして再送して頂けますか？	Can we ask you to send us supporting documents again in PDF format for individual September sales transactions that exceeded JPY 100 million?
4.2	9月の1億円を超える売上取引の根拠資料はありますが、そろえるのに時間がかかりそうです。	We have supporting documents for individual September sales transactions that exceeded JPY 100 million. However, it will take time to organize them.
4.3	9月の1億円を超える売上取引の根拠資料を誰に送ったか教えて頂けますか？	To whom did you send the supporting documents for individual September sales transactions that exceeded JPY 100 million?
4.4	8月と比較した9月の売上増の理由を知りたいのですが、1億円を超える売上取引の根拠資料はありますか？	Do you have any supporting documents for individual sales transactions that exceeded JPY 100 million as we would like to know the reason for the increase in sales in September as compared with August?
4.5	何度も督促して申し訳ありませんが、9月の1億円を超える売上取引の根拠資料はありますか？	We apologize for bothering you so much, but could you provide us supporting documents for individual September sales transactions that exceeded JPY 100 million?

Case 40 売上計上の遅れの理由を確認する

基本文

	日本語	英　語
5	今月の<u>A社への売上計上</u>が遅れているのはなぜでしょうか？	Why is <u>the posting of sales from A company</u> behind schedule this month?

A社からの入金（payment from A company）
A社との契約書の最終化（finalization of the contract with A company）
関係会社残高差異調整（reconciliation of intercompany balance variance）
月次報告（monthly report）
特許権使用料の計算書（patent royalty calculation sheet）

展開文

	日本語	英　語
5.1	今月のA社への売上計上が遅れている理由をご教示下さい。	Could explain the reason why the posting of sales from A company is behind schedule this month?
5.2	今月のA社への売上計上は遅れているのは，A社からの検収書の入手が遅れているためです。	The posting of sales from A company is behind schedule because we have not received the acceptance certificate from them yet.
5.3	今月のA社への売上計上は遅れる見込みというのは確かでしょうか？	Is it true that the posting of sales from A Company will be delayed this month?
5.4	教えて頂けるとありがたいのですが，今月のA社への売上計上が遅れているのはなぜでしょうか？	It would be appreciated if you could explain why the posting of sales from A company is behind schedule this month.
5.5	今月のA社への売上計上が遅れている理由について，遅くとも次の金曜日までにご回答下さい。	Please let us know by next Friday at the latest the reason why the posting of sales from A company is behind schedule this month.

2　購買に関する質問・回答

Case 41　購買依頼申請書の内容に関して質問する

基本文

	日本語	英 語
1	<u>購買依頼申請書</u>の内容に関して質問があります。	We have a question about the <u>purchase request form</u>.

稟議書（Ringi（circular letter））　　未着品（goods in-transit）
買掛金残高明細（AP breakdown）　　未払金（accounts payable）
見積書（quote）　　棚卸資産回転期間（inventory turnover period）
納品書（delivery slip）　　仕入の期間帰属（purchase cut off）
買掛金の年齢表（AP aging list）　　車両運搬具の購入（purchase of vehicle）

展開文

	日本語	英 語
1.1	購買依頼申請書の内容に関して，以下の点についてお伺い致します。	We would like to ask you the following questions about the purchase request form.
1.2	購買依頼申請書の内容に関しては山田さんに聞いて下さい。	Please ask Yamada-san about the purchase request form.
1.3	3日前に購買依頼申請書の内容に関して質問しましたが，ご回答頂いておりません。	We have not received your response regarding the questions related to the purchase request form that we sent to you three days ago.
1.4	購買依頼申請書の備考欄の記載内容に関して質問があります。	We have a question about the notes on the purchase request form.
1.5	ブラジルのビジネスの実務に詳しくないのですが，購買依頼申請書の内容に関して質問があります。	I have a question about the description in purchase request form as I am not familiar with the business practices in Brazil.

Case 42　発注数量の誤りの可能性について問い合わせる

基本文

	日本語	英　語
2	<u>発注数量</u>の入力を誤るという可能性はありますか？	**Is there any possibility that there are input errors in the <u>order quantity</u>?**

発注単価（unit price）
発注先の住所（vendor address）
送付先（delivery address）
請求書の記載内容（information on the invoice）
仕入値引（purchase discount）
帳簿価額（book value）
手数料の計算（calculation of commission）

展開文

	日本語	英　語
2.1	発注数量の入力を誤るというリスクに対して、どのように対処していますか？	How do you control the risk of input errors in order quantity?
2.2	どうして発注数量が違ってしまっているのでしょうか？	Why was the order quantity incorrect?
2.3	既存のシステムの設定上は、発注数量の入力を誤る可能性があるということでしょうか？	Does it mean that there is a possibility of inputting the wrong order quantity with the existing system settings?
2.4	A製品の発注数量の入力を誤るという可能性はありますか？	Is there any possibility that there are some input errors in the order quantity for product A?
2.5	9月の買掛金残高が大幅に増加しているのですが、発注数量の入力を誤ったという可能性はありますか？	The September AP balance increased significantly in comparison with August. Is there any possibility that there were some input errors in the order quantity?

Case 43　購買仕訳の入力者に関する理解を確認する

基本文

	日本語	英　語
3	<u>購買</u>に関する仕訳は経理部が入力しているという理解でよろしいでしょうか？	Is my understanding correct that the accounting department makes <u>purchase</u> journal entries?

固定資産（fixed assets）　　未払費用（accrued expense）
引当金（provisions）　　現金（cash）
企業結合（business combinations）　　建設仮勘定（construction in progress）
持分法（equity method）　　個別原価計算（job costing）
ヘッジ会計（hedge accounting）　　社債発行費（bond issuance costs）

展開文

	日本語	英　語
3.1	購買に関する仕訳を入力している部署はどこでしょうか？	Which department records journal entries for purchases?
3.2	購買に関する仕訳を入力している部署は経理部です。	The accounting department records journal entries for purchases.
3.3	購買に関する仕訳は入力済みでしょうか？	Have you recorded journal entries for purchases yet?
3.4	購買に関する仕訳は，経理部ではなく調達部が入力しているという理解でよろしいでしょうか？	Does the procurement department record journal entries for purchases, not the accounting department?
3.5	貴社が作成した買掛金残高確認書に誤りがあるように見受けられるのですが，購買に関する仕訳は経理部が入力しているという理解でよろしいでしょうか？	The AP confirmation you prepared appears to be incorrect. Is my understanding correct that the accounting department makes purchase journal entries?

Case 44 移転価格を考慮しているかどうかについて問い合わせる

基本文

	日本語	英語
4	関連当事者との取引においては，<u>移転価格</u>を考慮していますか？	Do you take <u>transfer pricing</u> into consideration when entering into related party transactions?

タックス・ヘイブン対策税制（Anti-Tax Haven Rules）
過少資本税制（Thin Capitalization Rules）
日米租税条約（Japan-U.S. Tax Treaty）
恒久的施設（Permanent Establishment（PE））
外国税額控除（Foreign Tax Credit）

展開文

	日本語	英語
4.1	関連当事者との取引においては，移転価格を考慮していなければ，税務上のリスクが生じます。	You may bear a risk of tax errors if you do not take transfer pricing into consideration when entering into related party transactions.
4.2	関連当事者との取引において，移転価格を考慮しなければならないことは十分承知しています。	We all understand that we have to take transfer pricing into consideration when entering into related party transactions.
4.3	関連当事者との取引においては，移転価格を考慮することにご留意下さい。	Please make sure to take transfer pricing into consideration when entering into related party transactions.
4.4	関連当事者との取引においては，移転価格を考慮して，独立企業間価格で価格を設定する必要があります。	We have to take transfer pricing into consideration to determine the prices are at arm's length when entering into related party transactions.
4.5	税務当局からの問い合わせに関連する質問ですが，関連当事者との取引においては，移転価格を考慮していますか？	This is a follow up question from the tax agency. Do you take transfer pricing into consideration when determining the prices of related party transactions?

Case 45　関係会社残高確認の差異分析結果を送ってもらう

基本文

	日本語	英　語
5	<u>関係会社残高確認の差異分析の結果</u>を今日中にご連絡頂くことはできますか？	Would it be possible for us to have the <u>results of your intercompany balance variance analysis</u> today?

返品数量（number of goods returned）
最終の検査書（final inspection report）
固定資産台帳（fixed assets register）
定款（article of incorporation）
売掛金貸方残高の内容（details of credit balance of AR）
買掛金借方残高の内容（details of debit balance of AP）

展開文

	日本語	英　語
5.1	関係会社残高確認の差異分析の調査結果のご連絡は，今日が締切りとなっています。	Please note today is the reporting deadline for the results of the intercompany balance variance analysis.
5.2	関係会社残高確認の差異分析の結果のご連絡を，明日まで延期することはできますか？	Would it be possible to extend the reporting deadline for the results of the intercompany balance variance analysis until tomorrow?
5.3	関係会社残高確認の差異分析の調査結果を昨日までにご連絡頂けるはずでしたが，状況いかがでしょうか？	We have not received the results of the intercompany balance variance analysis from you. What is the status?
5.4	残高確認の差異分析の結果を現地時間の今日中にご連絡頂くことはできますか？	Would it be possible for us to have the results of your intercompany balance variance analysis by today your time?
5.5	関係会社残高確認の差異を調整するため，分析の結果を今日中にご連絡頂くことはできますか？	Would it be possible for us to have the results of your intercompany balance variance analysis today so that we will be able to perform the reconciliation?

3　入出金に関する質問・回答

Case 46　送金が完了しているかどうかについて問い合わせる

基本文

	日本語	英　語
1	8月分の<u>送金</u>は完了していますか？	Has the <u>remittance</u> for August been completed?

送金振込（electronic transfer）
口座引き落とし（bank withdrawal）
銀行残高調整（bank reconciliation）
資金繰り表（cash flow statement）
現金出納帳（cashbook）
仮入金の返済（repayment of loan）

展開文

	日本語	英　語
1.1	8月分が送金済みかどうかご確認頂けますか？	Can you please double check whether the remittance for August has been completed?
1.2	8月分の送金は完了しています。	The remittance for August has been completed and submitted.
1.3	通常であれば、8月分の送金は9月3日には到着しているはずです。	Normally, the remittance for August should have reached you by September 3.
1.4	8月分の経営指導料に関する送金は完了していますか？	Has the management fee remittance for August been completed?
1.5	これで2回目の督促ですが、8月分の送金は完了していますか？	This is the second follow up. Has the remittance for August been completed?

Case 47　送金に関する法律上の制限の有無について確認する

基本文

	日本語	英　語
2	送金に関して，現地で<u>何らかの法律上の制限</u>はありますか？	Are there any <u>local legal restrictions</u> relating to the remittance in your country?

何らかの書類の要求（any document requirements）
送金限度額（the remittance limit）
何らかの事前許可の要求（any pre-approval requirements）
外貨持出し制限（the remittance limit on certain currencies）
何らかの免除（any exemptions）

展開文

	日本語	英　語
2.1	送金に関して，現地で法律上の制限を設けている目的は何でしょうか？	What is the purpose of the local legal restrictions relating to the remittance in your country?
2.2	送金に関する法律上の制限は特にありません。	There are no legal restrictions relating to the remittance.
2.3	送金に関する法律上の制限はいつごろ解除されるとお考えでしょうか？	Do you know when the legal restrictions relating to the remittance will be removed?
2.4	素朴な疑問ですが，送金に関して，現地で何か法律上の制限はありますか？	Just a quick question. Are there any local legal restrictions relating to the remittance in your country?
2.5	送金に関して，たとえば監督官庁の承認が求められるなど，現地で何か法律上の制限はありますか？	Are there any local legal restrictions relating to the remittance in your country such as mandatory approval by regulatory authorities?

Case 48　支払条件について質問する

基本文

	日本語	英　語
3	<u>支払条件</u>について質問があります。	We have a question about the <u>payment terms</u>.

決済期日（settlement date）
当座貸越の限度額（overdraft limit）
円安の影響（impact by depreciation of yen）
送金の目的（purpose of remittance）
融資限度額（line of credit）
財務制限違反（financial covenant violation）

展開文

	日本語	英　語
3.1	支払いを1か月延期することは可能でしょうか？	Is it possible to extend the payment by one month?
3.2	支払条件について質問があれば，何でも聞いて下さい。	Should you have any questions about the payment terms, please feel free to ask me.
3.3	支払条件を20日締め，翌月末払いに変更する件について，ご検討頂く機会はありましたでしょうか？	Have you had a chance to consider changing the payment terms that all invoices coming in up to the 20th day of each month will be paid at the end of the following month?
3.4	貴社から弊社への支払時期は翌月で結構ですが，支払条件について追加で質問があります。	We can accept your payment to be following month but we have another question about your payment terms.
3.5	支払いの手続を行いたいのですが，支払条件について質問があります。	We have a question about the payment terms as I would like to process the payment.

Case 49　口座番号を確認する

基本文

	日本語	英　語
4	貴社の口座番号は12345678で正しいですよね？	Is <u>your bank account number 12345678?</u>

金融機関コード（ABA number／IBAN／Sort Code）

展開文

	日本語	英　語
4.1	我々の取引銀行から，貴社の口座番号12345678に送金できないという連絡がありました。	We were informed by our bank that they could not process an electronic transfer to your bank account number 12345678.
4.2	口座番号は12345678ではなく，98765432です。	Our bank account number is not 12345678. It is 98765432.
4.3	新しい口座番号12345678はいつから有効になりますか？	When will your new bank account number 12345678 be effective?
4.4	送金する口座番号は12345678と98765432のどちらがよろしいでしょうか？	Which bank account number is preferable for the remittance, 12345678 or 98765432?
4.5	念のための確認ですが，口座番号は12345678で正しいですよね？	Just to clarify, your bank account number is 12345678, correct?

Chapter IV　場面別　メール表現

Case 50　送金の内訳について問い合わせる

基本文

	日本語	英 語
5	<u>11月22日の送金の内訳</u>を教えて頂けますか？	Could you please send us the <u>breakdown of the remittance on November 22</u>?

権利放棄証書の詳細（details of waiver）
未払利息の内訳（breakdown of accrued interest）
シンジケーション手数料の内訳（breakdown of syndication fee）
借り換えを予定している短期借入金の内訳（breakdown of short-term loans expected to be refinanced on a long-term basis）
仮勘定の内訳（breakdown of suspense account）
運転資金残高（working capital balance）
リスク・フリー・レート（risk free rate）

展開文

	日本語	英 語
5.1	11月22日の送金の内訳は作成していますか？	Have you prepared the breakdown of the remittance on November 22?
5.2	11月22日の送金の内訳は作成次第お送り致します。	We will send you the breakdown of the remittance on November 22 as soon as it is prepared.
5.3	いったいいつになったら11月22日の送金の内訳を教えて頂けるのでしょうか？	How soon can we receive the breakdown of the remittance on November 22 from you?
5.4	11月22日の送金の目的を明確にしたいのですが，内訳を教えて頂けますか？	We would like to know the purpose of the remittance on November 22. Could you please send us a breakdown of the remittance?
5.5	監査人から11月22日の送金の目的に関する問い合わせを受けていますので，内訳を教えて頂けますか？	We were asked by our auditor about the purpose of the remittance on November 22. Could you please send us the breakdown of the remittance?

4　人件費（その他）に関する質問・回答

Case 51　給与テーブルの変更の有無を確認する

基本文

	日本語	英　語
1	<u>給与テーブル</u>を昨年から変更しましたか？	Did you change <u>your payroll table</u> from last year?

給与の支払日（the payday）
給与計算期間（the payroll period）
給与計算システム（the payroll system）
給与計算業者（the payroll service provider）
給与規定（the payroll policy）

展開文

	日本語	英　語
1.1	いつ給与テーブルを変更しましたか？	When did you change your payroll table?
1.2	給与テーブルを少しだけ変更しました。	We made a minor change on our payroll table.
1.3	近い将来給与テーブルを変更する予定はありますか？	Are you going to change your payroll table in the near future?
1.4	駐在員の給与テーブルを昨年から変更しましたか？	Did you change your expats payroll table from last year?
1.5	以前も伺っていたらすいませんが，給与テーブルを昨年から変更しましたか？	Sorry if we asked you the same question before but did you change your payroll table from last year?

Case 52　弁護士の見解の入手の有無について問い合わせる

基本文

	日本語	英　語
2	<u>弁護士の見解</u>は入手していますか？	**Have you obtained <u>a legal opinion</u>?**

　　顧問弁護士の見解（an opinion of legal counsel）
　　和解提案（a settlement proposal）
　　集団訴訟の訴状（a class action notice）
　　事業価値評価レポート（the valuation report）
　　資産評価（PPA）レポート（Purchase Price Allocation（PPA）report）
　　監査報告書（an audit report）

展開文

	日本語	英　語
2.1	弁護士の見解を入手するのにはどれくらいかかりそうですか？	How long will it take to obtain a legal opinion?
2.2	今回は弁護士の見解は入手していません。	We did not obtain a legal opinion this time.
2.3	もうすでに弁護士の見解を入手していなければならない時期だと思います。	We think it is time to obtain a legal opinion.
2.4	得意先から受けた訴訟案件に関する弁護士の見解は入手していますか？	Have you obtained a legal opinion regarding the lawsuit with the customer?
2.5	毎度のことですが，弁護士の見解を入手して頂けますか？	Will you please obtain a legal opinion as usual?

Case 53　税務調査の指摘事項に関する見解について問い合わせる

基本文

	日本語	英　語
3	<u>税務調査における指摘事項</u>について，どのようにお考えでしょうか？	What is your view regarding <u>the items noted by the investigator during the tax investigation</u>?

顧問税理士の見解（opinion of your tax advisor）
交際費の損金算入の可能性（deductibility of entertainment expenses for tax purposes）
課徴金の支払いの可能性（probability of fines）
不正の再発防止策（measures to prevent recurrence/reoccurrence of fraud）
内部通報制度の有効性（effectiveness of whistle-blower system）
監査役のコメント（comments of the corporate auditors）
偶発事象（contingency）
粉飾決算の可能性（probability of window dressing）

展開文

	日本語	英　語
3.1	税務調査における指摘事項に関する貴社の見解について納得できません。	I'm not convinced by your explanation regarding the items noted by the investigator during the tax investigation.
3.2	税務調査における指摘事項には全く合理性がないと考えています。調査官が参照している条文を教えて下さい。	We think the items noted by the investigator during the tax investigation are totally unreasonable. Please tell us which section in the Code the inspector refers to.
3.3	税務調査における指摘事項について，お考えをお聞かせ頂いていたでしょうか？	Have we heard your view regarding items noted by the investigator during the tax investigation?
3.4	先月実施された税務調査における指摘事項について，どのようにお考えでしょうか？	What is your view regarding the items noted by the investigator during the tax investigation executed last month?
3.5	税務上のリスクを把握したいのですが，税務調査における指摘事項について，どのようにお考えでしょうか？	Could you share your view regarding the items noted by the investigator during the tax investigation? We would like to know any tax related risks.

Case 54　移転価格税制に関する事前確認が完了しているかどうかについて問い合わせる

基本文

	日本語	英　語
4	<u>移転価格税制に関する事前確認(APA)</u>が完了しているかどうかご存知ですか？	Do you know if <u>the Advance Pricing Agreement (APA)</u> has been completed yet?

租税条約に関する届出書の提出（submission of the Income Tax Convention application form）

税務申告書の提出（filing of tax return）

自己申告（リニエンシー）の申請（application of leniency program）

現地会計基準とIFRSの差異の調査（investigation of differences between the local GAAP and IFRS）

損金算入費用のレビュー（review of tax-deductible expenses）

展開文

	日本語	英　語
4.1	APAは完了しているかどうかご教示頂けますか？	Could you please advise us if the APA has been completed yet?
4.2	現時点ではAPAは完了していません。	The APA has not been completed yet.
4.3	今月中にAPAを完了させることは可能でしょうか？	Will you be able to complete the APA this month?
4.4	米国子会社との取引に係るAPAが完了しているかどうかご存知ですか？	Do you know if the APA relating to transactions with the U.S. subsidiaries has been completed yet?
4.5	あなたのご担当ではないかもしれませんが，APAが完了しているかどうかご存知ですか？	You may not be the right person to ask, but do you know if the APA has been completed yet?

Case 55 監査人による監査が終了していない理由を確認する

基本文

	日本語	英　語
5	<u>監査人</u>による<u>監査</u>が終了していないのはなぜでしょうか？	Why has <u>the audit</u> not been completed yet?

第三者委員会による不正調査（the fraud investigation by the independent committee）
関係会社残高差異調整（the reconciliation of intercompany balance variance）
会計事務所による財務デューデリジェンス（the financial Due Diligence procedures by the accounting firm）
法律事務所による法務デューデリジェンス（the legal Due Diligence procedures by the law firm）
期中監査（interim audit）
監査手続（the audit procedure）
業務監査（the operational audit）

展開文

	日本語	英　語
5.1	監査人による監査がまだ終了していないのではないですか？	Hasn't the audit been completed yet?
5.2	正直に言うと，有形固定資産の評価について見解の相違があり，監査人による監査が終了していません。	To be honest, the audit has not been completed yet due to the difference in PP&E evaluation between the Company and the auditor.
5.3	いつ監査人による監査が終了すると期待していますか？	When do you expect the auditor to complete the audit?
5.4	監査人による現地法定財務諸表の監査が終了していないのはなぜでしょうか？　4月20日までに終了しないと，大変な問題になります。	Why has the local statutory audit not been completed yet? It will cause a serious problem if you fail to make the audit completed by April 20.
5.5	今年は監査の終了が例年より遅れているようですが，監査人による監査が終了していないのはなぜでしょうか？	The audit seems to be behind schedule this year. Do you know why the audit has not been completed yet?

5 予算に関する質問・回答

Case 56　予算案が取締役会で承認されたものかどうかについて確認する

基本文

	日本語	英 語
1	<u>予算案</u>は取締役会で承認されたものでしょうか？	Is the <u>budget plan</u> approved at the board of directors meeting?

中期（長期）経営計画（medium-term（long-term）management plan）
事業計画（business plan）　減資（capital reduction）
新株発行（issuance of new shares）　企業再編計画（reorganization plan）
社債発行（issuance of corporate bonds）　出資（capital injection）
技術提携契約（Technical Collaboration Agreement）
流動比率（current ratio）　子会社の設立（incorporation of a subsidiary）
負債資本比率（debt to equity ratio）　清算計画（liquidation plan）

展開文

	日本語	英 語
1.1	予算案は，お送り頂く前に取締役会で承認を得る必要があります。	The budget plan needs to be approved at the board of directors meeting before submission.
1.2	予算案は，取締役会ではなくCFOが承認したものになります。	The budget plan is approved by the CFO not at the board of directors meeting.
1.3	予算案は，いつ取締役会で承認されますか？	When will the board of directors approve the budget?
1.4	昨日お送り頂いた予算案は取締役会で承認されたものでしょうか？	Was the budget plan submitted yesterday approved at the board of directors meeting?
1.5	簡単な質問ですが，予算案は取締役会で承認されたものでしょうか？	This is a quick question. Is the budget plan approved at the board of directors meeting?

Case 57　予算に対する実績の進捗状況について問い合わせる

基本文

	日本語	英　語
2	<u>上半期の予算</u>に対する実績の進捗状況はいかがでしょうか？	How was the actual results compare to the <u>budget for the 1st half</u>?

第1四半期の予算（budget for the 1st quarter）
下半期の予算（budget for the 2nd half）
2017年3月期会計年度の予算（budget for the fiscal year ending March 31, 2017）

展開文

	日本語	英　語
2.1	上半期の予算に対して実績は順調ですか？	Are the actual results comparing favorably with the budget in the 1st half?
2.2	上半期の予算に対して実績の進捗は芳しくありません。	The actual results are under the expected budget in the 1st half.
2.3	下半期の予算に対する実績はどのようになる見通しでしょうか？	How do you expect the results to compare to the budget in the 2nd half?
2.4	2015年度上半期の予算に対する実績の進捗はいかがでしょうか？	What is the progress to achieving the budget in the 1st half of FY2015?
2.5	回答が難しいかもしれませんが，上半期の予算に対する実績の進捗状況はいかがでしょうか？	This may be difficult to answer but what is the progress on achieving the budget in the 1st half?

Case 58 売上高を増やす余地の有無について問い合わせる

基本文

	日本語	英語
3	<u>大口の新規顧客を獲得する</u>余地はありますか？	Is there any chance to <u>win large new customers</u>?

経費を減らす（reduce expenses）
広告宣伝費を減らす（reduce advertising expenses）
交際費を減らす（reduce entertainment expenses）
旅費交通費を減らす（reduce travel expenses）
通信費を減らす（reduce communication expenses）
直接費を減らす（reduce direct costs）
間接費を減らす（reduce indirect costs）
利息費用を減らす（reduce interest expense）
小口現金残高を減らす（reduce the balance of petty cash）

展開文

	日本語	英語
3.1	大口の新規顧客を獲得する方策のご検討をお願いできますか？	May we ask you to take measures to win new large customers?
3.2	予算案は現実的なものであり，大口の新規顧客を獲得する余地はありません。	Our budget plan is realistic and we see no chance to win large new customers.
3.3	新製品を予定より早く投入することにより，大口の新規顧客を獲得することができるかもしれません。	It may be possible to win large new customers by launching new products earlier than originally scheduled.
3.4	貴社の予算案は少し保守的なように思われますが，大口の新規顧客を獲得する余地はありますか？	Is there any chance of winning large new customers as your budget plan seems a little conservative?
3.5	過去の経験にとらわれずに，大口の新規顧客を獲得する余地があるかどうか，ご検討頂けますか？	Past experiences aside, could you please consider if there is any chance of winning large new customers?

2 子会社，取引先等への質問・回答

Case 59　売上高が下回っている原因について問い合わせる

基本文

	日本語	英　語
4	3月の<u>売上高</u>が予算を下回っている原因は何でしょうか？	What is the reason that <u>sales</u> in March are below the budget target?

売上原価（cost of sales）
販売費および一般管理費（selling, general and administrative expenses）
減価償却費（depreciation expenses）
受取利息（interest income）
支払利息（interest expense）
貸倒損失（bad debt expense）
営業成績（operating results）
経常利益（income from continuing operation）
研究開発費（R&D expense）
付加価値税（value-added tax（VAT））

展開文

	日本語	英　語
4.1	3月の売上高が予算に比べて足りない原因について分析してもらえますか？	Would it be possible to analyze the reason that sales in March are below the budget target?
4.2	3月に見込んでいた製品の出荷が4月にずれたため、3月の売上高が予算未達となりました。	Sales in March were below the budget target as the expected shipment of products in March was postponed to April.
4.3	3月の売上高が予算に比べて足りない原因を今週中に報告して頂けますか？	Would you please report the reason by this weekend why sales in March are below the budget target?
4.4	3月の売上高が予算に比べて10%足りない原因は何でしょうか？	What is the reason that sales in March are below the budget target by 10%?
4.5	3月の売上高が予算に比べて1,000万円足りない原因は何でしょうか？	What is the reason that sales in March are below the budget target by JPY 10 million?

Case 60 レポーティングパッケージの入力内容が一致しない理由について問い合わせる

基本文

	日本語	英語
5	<u>レポーティングパッケージのフォームAとフォームBの金額が一致しないのはなぜでしょうか？</u>	Could you please explain the reason the amount in form A does not agree with the amount in form B in <u>the reporting package</u>?

退職給付債務の見積り（estimation of Projected Benefit Obligation（PBO））
賞与の計算式（calculation of bonus）
使用すべきフォーム（the forms to be used）
フリーキャッシュフローの計算方法（calculation method of Free Cash Flow（FCF））
レポーティングパッケージの送付先（addressee of the reporting package）
課税所得の計算（calculation of taxable income）

展開文

	日本語	英語
5.1	レポーティングパッケージの入力にいくつか誤りがあるように見受けられます。	It seems that there are some input errors in the reporting package.
5.2	申し訳ありません。誤りですので、すぐに訂正致します。	We are sorry. We will correct it immediately as it is a mistake.
5.3	レポーティングパッケージの誤りは、4月10日まで修正することができます。	We will correct the error in the reporting package before April 10.
5.4	来年度予算のレポーティングパッケージの入力に誤りがあるように見受けられます。	It seems that there is an error in input of the budget for next fiscal year in the reporting package.
5.5	私の勘違いかもしれませんが、レポーティングパッケージの入力に誤りがあるように見受けられます。	I might be wrong, but it seems that there is an error in input of the reporting package.

6 決算に関する質問・回答

Case 61 繰延税金資産残高の増加理由について問い合わせる

基本文

	日本語	英　語
1	3月末の<u>繰延税金資産の残高</u>が，前月末と比べて増加している理由についてご説明頂けますか？	Could you please explain the reason why <u>the balance in deferred tax assets</u> as of the end of March increased compared to that as of the end of last month?

有形固定資産残高（balance in Property, Plant and Equipment (PP&E)）
無形資産（intangible assets）
貸倒引当金（allowance for doubtful accounts）
有給休暇引当金（accrued vacation payable）
実効税率（effective income tax rate）
繰越欠損金（tax loss carry forward）
将来加算一時差異（future taxable temporary difference）
将来減算一時差異（future deductible temporary difference）

展開文

	日本語	英　語
1.1	3月末の繰延税金資産の残高が，前月末と比べて増加している理由についてもう少し情報を下さい。	Could you give us more information about the reason why the balance in deferred tax assets as of the end of March increased compared to that as of the end of last month?
1.2	3月末の繰延税金資産の残高が，前年同月末と比べて減少している理由についてご説明頂けますか？	Could you please explain the reason why the balance in deferred tax assets as of the end of March decreased compared to that as of the end of last month?
1.3	3月末の繰延税金資産の残高が，前月末と比べて増加している理由については既にご説明頂いていましたでしょうか？	Have you already explained the reason why the balance in deferred tax assets as of the end of March increased compared to that as of the end of last month?

1.4	3月末の繰延税金資産の残高が，前月末と比べて大幅に増加している理由についてご説明頂けますか？	Could you please explain the reason why the balance in deferred tax assets as of the end of March increased significantly compared to that as of the end of last month?
1.5	繰越欠損金に重要な変動がないにもかかわらず，繰延税金資産の残高が前年度末と比べて増加している理由についてご説明頂けますか？	Could you please explain the reason why the balance in deferred tax assets increased compared to the prior year end balance despite no significant movement in net operating loss carry forwards?

Case 62　修正仕訳を入力してよいかどうか確認する

基本文

	日本語	英　語
2	<u>修正仕訳</u>は私たちのほうで入力しましょうか？	Should we input <u>the adjusting entry</u>?

連結消去仕訳（consolidation elimination entries）
未実現利益消去仕訳（entries to eliminate unrealized profit）
債権債務消去仕訳（entries to eliminate intercompany debts and credits）
投資と資本の消去仕訳（entries to eliminate investment and capital）
手仕訳（manual entries）
期首残高修正仕訳（adjusting entry to the opening balance）
期末残高修正仕訳（adjusting entry to the closing balance）

展開文

	日本語	英　語
2.1	修正仕訳は私たちのほうで入力することをご希望ですか？	Would you like us to input the adjusting entry on our side?
2.2	修正仕訳は私たちが入力するのと，貴社で入力するのとどちらがよいですか？	Who do you prefer to input the adjusting entry, you or us?
2.3	修正仕訳はあなた方のほうで入力して頂けますと幸いです。	We would appreciate it if you could input the adjusting entry.
2.4	修正仕訳がまだ入力されていないようですが，私たちのほうで入力しましょうか？	It seems that the adjusting entry has not been recorded yet. Should we make it on our side?
2.5	昨日指摘した修正仕訳はグループレベルで私たちのほうで入力します。貴社の単体決算では，翌年度で修正して下さい。	We input the adjusting entry at group level that we pointed out yesterday. For your statutory financial closing, please input necessary adjusting entry in the following year.

Case 63 棚卸資産の実地棚卸が必要かどうか確認する

基本文

	日本語	英　語
3	わたしたちの会社は期末日での<u>棚卸資産の実地棚卸</u>をする必要はありますか？	Do we have to perform a <u>physical inventory count</u> as of fiscal year end date?

残高確認（balance confirmation）
過剰在庫の分析（analysis of excess inventory）
金庫の現物確認（physical inspection of a safe box）
正味実現可能価額の分析（analysis of net realizable value）
のれんの減損テスト（impairment test of goodwill）
繰延税金資産の回収可能性の検討（evaluation of the recoverability of deferred tax assets）
差異分析（variance analysis）
固定資産の実地棚卸（fixed assets count）
継続企業の前提に関する評価（assessment of our entity's ability to continue as a going concern）

展開文

	日本語	英　語
3.1	わたしたちの会社は期末日での棚卸資産の実地棚卸の対象会社ですか？	Are we subject to a physical inventory count as of fiscal year end date?
3.2	外部倉庫保管分についても，棚卸資産の実地棚卸をする必要はありますか？	Do we have to perform a physical inventory count on third party warehouse's?
3.3	わたしたちの会社は従来期末日に棚卸資産の実地棚卸をしてこなかったのですが，今年度から実施をする必要はありますか？	Do we have to perform a physical inventory count as of fiscal year end date although we have never done so in the past?
3.4	重要性がないにもかかわらず，期末日に棚卸資産の実地棚卸をする必要はありますか？	Do we have to perform a physical inventory count as of fiscal year end date even if immateriality?
3.5	わたしたちの会社は年２回も棚卸資産の実地棚卸をする必要はありますか？	Do we have to perform a physical inventory count semi-annually?

Case 64　引当金の見積りに使用した前提条件について問い合わせる

基本文

	日本語	英　語
4	<u>製品保証引当金</u>の見積りに使用した前提条件は何でしょうか？	What assumptions did you use in estimating <u>the product warranty provision</u>?

貸倒引当金（allowance for doubtful accounts）　　返品引当金（sales return provision）
リストラ引当金（restructuring provision）　　環境対策引当金（environmental provision）
資産除去債務（asset retirement obligation）　　繰延収益（deferred revenue）
金融負債の現在価値（present value of financial liabilities）
在庫の市場価格（market value of inventory）　　経済的耐用年数（economic useful life）
金融資産の公正価値（fair value of financial assets）
期待運用収益率（expected rate of return）　　減損損失（impairment loss）

展開文

	日本語	英　語
4.1	製品保証引当金の見積りに使用した前提条件を教えて下さい。	Please explain assumptions you used in estimating the product warranty provision.
4.2	製品保証引当金の見積りに使用した前提条件は添付のとおりです。	Assumptions we used in estimating the product warranty provision are as attached.
4.3	製品保証引当金の見積りに使用した前提条件は何か，できるだけ早く教えて頂けますか？	Could you please explain what assumptions you used in estimating the product warranty provision as soon as possible?
4.4	注記に記載されている製品保証引当金の見積りに使用した前提条件についての詳細を教えて頂けますか？	Could you please explain what assumptions you used in estimating the product warranty provision disclosed in the footnote?
4.5	製品保証引当金の見積りに使用した前提条件が変更されているのは何故ですか？　また，昨年と同じ前提条件だといくらになりますか？	Could you please explain why you changed the assumptions you used in estimating the product warranty provision? Also, please tell us what amount we will have if you apply the same assumptions as you used in the prior year.

Chapter IV　場面別　メール表現

Case 65　その他の費用に何が含まれているかについて問い合わせる

基本文

	日本語	英　語
5	<u>その他の費用</u>には何が含まれていますか？	**What is included in <u>other expenses</u>?**

その他の収益（other income）
特別利益（extraordinary income）
特別損失（extraordinary expense）
その他の資産（other assets）
その他の負債（other liabilities）
税額控除（tax credit）
未経過利息（unearned interest）

展開文

	日本語	英　語
5.1	その他の費用の内訳を教えて下さい。	Please explain the breakdown of other expenses.
5.2	その他の費用の内訳は添付のとおりです。	The breakdown of other expenses is as attached.
5.3	その他の費用には何が含まれているか，できるだけ早く教えて頂けますか？	Could you please explain what is included in other expenses as soon as possible?
5.4	損益計算書に計上されているその他の費用には何が含まれていますか？	What is included in other expenses in the income statement?
5.5	環境対策費はその他の費用ではなく，一般管理費に計上すべきではないですか？	Should we include the environmental charges as general expenses rather than other expenses?

7 内部統制に関する質問・回答

Case 66　社内規定等を変更したかどうかを確認する

基本文

	日本語	英　語
1	当期から<u>社内規定</u>を変更しましたか？	Have your <u>corporate policies</u> been changed since last fiscal year?

業務記述書（business process description）
経理規程（Accounting Policy Manual（APM））
リスク管理規程（risk management policy）
組織図（organization chart）
職務権限表（delegation of authorization chart）
資金調達プロセス（financing process）
債務保証プロセス（financial guarantee process）

展開文

	日本語	英　語
1.1	当期から社内規定を変更したかどうかわかりますか？	Do you know whether your corporate policies have changed since last fiscal year?
1.2	いい質問ですね。当期から社内規定を変更しています。	That is a good question. We changed our corporate policies since last fiscal year.
1.3	来期から社内規定を変更する予定はありますか？	Will your corporate policies be changed from next fiscal year?
1.4	当期から内部通報制度に関する社内規定を変更しましたか？	Have your corporate policies on the whistle-blower system changed since last fiscal year?
1.5	厳密にいうと，当期に変更した社内規定は，来期から適用となります。	Strictly speaking, the corporate policies changes made this year will be effective from next fiscal year.

Case 67　内部統制の不備の改善方法について問い合わせる

基本文

	日本語	英語
2	内部統制の不備をどのように改善する予定でしょうか？	How do you remediate the control deficiency?

外注先の内部統制（internal controls at subcontractors）
販売システムと会計システムの自動連携（automated coordination of sales system and accounting system）
内部通報の仕組み（whistle-blower system）
全社統制の不備（deficiencies in entity level control）
IT全般統制の不備（deficiencies in IT general control）
債務免除益の計算の不備（deficiencies in discharge of indebtness income calculation）

展開文

	日本語	英語
2.1	内部統制の不備を改善するために，どのような対策をお考えでしょうか？	What measures are required to remediate the control deficiency?
2.2	12月までに改善策を決定し，2月から実践する予定です。	We will determine the action plan by December and implement it in February.
2.3	いつ内部統制の不備を改善する予定となっていましたか？	When were you planning to implement the control improvements?
2.4	先月のテストで検出された内部統制の不備をどのように改善する予定でしょうか？	What solutions are you developing for the control deficiency detected in the test conducted last month?
2.5	追加の質問ですが，内部統制の不備をどのように改善する予定でしょうか？　改善のための最大の障害は何でしょうか？	One more questions. What solutions are you developing for the control deficiencies and what is your biggest concern in remediating them?

2　子会社，取引先等への質問・回答

Case 68　テスト結果の文書化が完了しているかどうかについて問い合わせる

基本文

	日本語	英　語
3	<u>テスト結果の文書化</u>は完了していますか？	Has the <u>documentation of the test results</u> been completed?

決算業務の標準化（standardization of financial statement close process（FSCP））
経理部門のスキルアップ（improvement of skills of staff in the accounting department）
原価計算システムの導入（deployment of costing system）
固定資産の取得プロセスのテスト（test of fix assets procurement process）
統制不備要約表の作成（preparation of Summary of Control Deficiencies（SOCD））

展開文

	日本語	英　語
3.1	テスト結果の文書化が完了しているころと思い，メールしました。	I am writing this email to ask you if you have completed the testing.
3.2	テスト結果の文書化はおおむね完了しています。	The documentation of the test results has almost been completed.
3.3	テスト結果の文書化は2月までに完了する必要があります。	The documentation of the test results has to be completed by February.
3.4	先日お願いしていました，テスト結果の文書化は完了していますか？	Has the documentation of the test results, which we requested the other day, been completed?
3.5	監査人から要求されているのですが，テスト結果の文書化は完了していますか？	Our auditor requested us to provide the test results. Has the documentation of test results been completed?

Case 69 コントロールの内容について説明してもらう

基本文

	日本語	英 語
4	<u>コントロールNo.1の詳細内容について説明して頂けますか？</u>	**Could you please provide details of <u>control No. 1</u>?**

日次統制（daily controls）
月次統制（monthly controls）
四半期統制（quarterly controls）
半期統制（semi annual controls）
年次統制（annual controls）

展開文

	日本語	英 語
4.1	コントロールNo.1の内容がわからないのですが。	I could not understand your description of control No. 1.
4.2	コントロールNo.1は会計システムによるエラーチェック機能です。	Control No. 1 is the error check function in the accounting system.
4.3	コントロールNo.1の内容について次回のミーティング時に説明して頂けますか？	Could you please explain control No. 1 in the next meeting?
4.4	コントロールNo.1とコントロールNo.2の違いがわからないのですが，コントロールNo.1の内容について説明して頂けますか？	I do not understand the difference between Control No. 1 and Control No. 2, could you please explain Control No. 1 in more detail?
4.5	フローチャート上のコントロールNo.1の内容について説明して頂けますか？	Could you please describe control No. 1 in the flow chart?

Case 70　チェックマークの意味について問い合わせる

基本文

	日本語	英　語
5	このチェックマークは<u>上長がレビューした</u>という意味でしょうか？	Does this tick mark mean that <u>it was reviewed by the supervisor</u>?

テスト実施者がレビューした（it was reviewed by the person who performed the test）
経理部コントローラーが自ら記帳した（it was booked by Financial Controller (FC) himself/herself）
統制にエラーがあった（there was an error on the control）
経理部長が承認した（it was approved by the manager of the accounting department）
仕訳を入力した（journals were entered）

展開文

	日本語	英　語
5.1	ご理解のとおりです。このチェックマークは上長がレビューした証跡です。	Your understanding is correct. This tick mark means that it was reviewed by the supervisor.
5.2	上長はどのようにレビューを実施したのでしょうか？	How did the supervisor perform the review?
5.3	このチェックマークは担当者が確認したという意味ではなく，上長がレビューしたという意味です。	This tick mark does not mean that it was checked by the person in charge but reviewed by the supervisor.
5.4	この右上にあるチェックマークは上長がレビューしたという意味でしょうか？	Does this tick mark in the upper right corner mean that it was reviewed by the supervisor?
5.5	ちなみに，このチェックマークは上長がレビューしたという意味でしょうか？	By the way, does this tick mark mean that it was reviewed by the supervisor?

COFFEE BREAK

はい／いいえ　英語と日本語の返答の違い

　例えば，"Don't you need any help?"（「手伝いは必要ではないですか？」）という質問に対して，「はい，必要ではありません。」と回答したいとき，英語でどのように回答すればよいでしょうか。

　日本語の「はい，必要ではありません。」を英語に直訳しようとする場合，おそらく，"Yes, I don't."となりますが，これはよくある誤りです。正確には，"No, I don't."となります。日本語では質問自体に対して，「はい」「いいえ」を使い分けて回答するため，「はい，必要ではありません。」「いいえ，必要です。」となります。しかし，英語では質問されている内容自体に対して"Yes"か"No"で回答することになります。そのため，英語での回答は"Yes, I do."か"No, I don't."と"Yes""No"が日本語とは逆になります。ですので，慣れないうちは"Yes""No"の回答をする際には気をつけましょう。

（例）
Isn't he absent?（彼はお休みではないのですか。）
⇒Yes, he is.（いいえ，お休みです。）
　No, he isn't.（はい，お休みではありません。）
Didn't you attend the meeting?（会議に出席してなかったのですか。）
⇒Yes, I did.（いいえ，出席しました。）
　No, I didn't.（はい，出席してません。）
Won't you come with me?（一緒にこないのですか？）
⇒Yes, I will.（いいえ，いきます。）
　No, I won't.（はい，いきません。）

3 子会社，取引先等へのクレーム・対応

　日本の親会社担当者として，海外子会社の担当者とのコミュニケーションを行うにあたり，クレームが発生することは避けられないところです。具体的にクレームする側および受ける局面でどのような表現を使うのか，実際の例文を見てみましょう。

1 売上に関するクレーム・対応

Case 71　請求書の金額等の誤りを指摘する

基本文

	日本語	英　語
1	<u>請求書の金額</u>が間違っているようです。	It appears that the <u>invoiced amount</u> is incorrect.

請求書日付（date of invoice）　　販売インセンティブ（sales incentive）
請求先（client name on invoice）　見積書（sales quote）
支払期限（payment deadline）　　年齢表（aging list）
数量（quantity）

展開文

	日本語	英　語
1.1	A社への請求額に誤りがあるようです。	It appears that the amount invoiced to Company A is incorrect.
1.2	請求書の金額は正しくは450,000円ではないでしょうか？	Shouldn't the invoiced amount be JPY 450,000?
1.3	請求書の金額を今週末までに訂正して下さい。	The invoiced amount should be corrected by the end of this week.
1.4	請求書データは必ず確認するようにして下さい。	Please ensure that the invoice data is reviewed for accuracy.
1.5	得意先との関係が悪化する恐れがありますので，注意して下さい。	Please exercise care, as this could negatively impact our relationship with the customer.

Case 72　売上伝票等の遅れについて指摘する

基本文

	日本語	英　語
2	<u>売上伝票</u>が届いていません。	The <u>sales voucher</u> has not arrived yet.

入金伝票（receiving slip）
出金伝票（disbursement slip）
振替伝票（journal entry slip）
出荷報告書（shipping report）
請求書（invoice）

展開文

	日本語	英　語
2.1	売上伝票をまだ受け取っておりません。	We haven't received the sales voucher yet.
2.2	売上伝票は発送済みでしょうか？	Has the sales voucher been sent?
2.3	売上伝票は昨日までに受け取ることになっていました。	We were supposed to receive the sales voucher yesterday.
2.4	売上伝票はいつ準備できるのか教えて下さい。	Please tell us when the sales voucher will be ready.
2.5	営業部門担当者に至急連絡を取って下さい。	The sales division staff should be contacted immediately.

Case 73　出荷の遅れについて指摘する

基本文

	日本語	英 語
3	<u>出荷予定日</u>が過ぎていますので，至急対応して下さい。	The <u>scheduled shipping date</u> has passed. Please take immediate action.

納入期限（delivery deadline）
支払期日（payment deadline）
売掛金回収期間（trade receivable collection deadline）
サービス完了日（service completion date）
暫定のレポート提出日（preliminary report delivery date）

展開文

	日本語	英 語
3.1	出荷予定日は3日前でしたので，至急出荷して下さい。	The scheduled shipping date has passed for 3 days. Please ship immediately.
3.2	出荷が遅れていますので，至急対応してもらえますか？	Please action shipment immediately, as it is behind schedule?
3.3	出荷予定日が過ぎていますが，いつ出荷できるか教えて下さい。	The scheduled shipment date has passed. When can the shipment be made?
3.4	得意先から苦情が来ていますので，至急対応して下さい。	We are receiving complaints from our customer. Your immediate action is required.
3.5	出荷処理が遅れている原因を至急確認して下さい。	Why is the shipment delayed?

Case 74　売上帳の締めの遅れについて確認する

基本文

	日本語	英 語
4	現時点で<u>売上帳</u>が締まっていない理由を教えて下さい。	Why has <u>the sales subledger</u> not been closed yet?

仕入帳（purchase subledger）
売掛金補助簿（trade receivable subledger）
買掛金補助簿（trade payable subledger）

展開文

	日本語	英 語
4.1	売上帳がまだ締まっていないのは何故でしょうか？	Why hasn't the sales subledger been closed yet?
4.2	売上帳の締切が遅れている理由を教えて下さい。	Why has the closing of the sales subledger been delayed?
4.3	売上帳は先週末までに締められているはずでした。	The sales journal subledger should have been closed by the end of last week.
4.4	帳簿の締切が遅れそうなときは事前に連絡するようにして下さい。	Please notify us in advance when you anticipate delays in closing subledgers.
4.5	時間がありませんので，早急にフォローアップをして下さい。	Please follow up immediately, as time is limited.

Case 75　売掛金残高明細のセルフチェックを依頼する

基本文

	日本語	英語
5	<u>売掛金残高明細</u>に誤りがありました。提出前にセルフチェックをして下さい。	There was an error in the <u>detail report of trade receivables</u>. Please check the report prior to submission.

買掛金残高明細（detail report of trade payable）
商品残高明細（detail report of inventories）
受取手形明細（breakdown of notes receivable）
短期貸付金の明細（detail report of short-term loans receivables）
短期借入金の明細（detail report of short-term borrowings）
長期借入金の明細（detail report of long-term borrowings）
不良債権の明細（breakdown of bad debts）
不良在庫の明細（detail report of goods impaired by damage/deterioration）
約束手形の明細（breakdown of promissory note）
会計帳簿（accounting book）
流動資産の明細（detail report of current assets）
流動負債の明細（detail report of current liabilities）

展開文

	日本語	英語
5.1	提出前に，売掛金残高明細のセルフチェックを徹底します。	We will thoroughly check the detail report of trade receivables before submitting it.
5.2	提出前に，売掛金残高明細に誤りがないことを確認致します。	We will confirm that there are no errors in the detail report of trade receivables before submitting it.
5.3	提出前に，売掛金残高明細をセルフチェックするべきでした。	We should have checked the detail report of trade receivables before submitting it.
5.4	売掛金残高明細のチェック体制を見直します。	We will reconsider the checking procedures for the detail report of trade receivables.
5.5	売掛金残高明細は，時間的に余裕をもって作成するようにします。	The detail report of trade receivables will be created well in advance.

2 購買に関するクレーム・対応

Case 76　購買依頼書等の処理の遅れを指摘する

基本文

	日本語	英語
1	営業所から回付された<u>購買依頼書</u>の処理が1か月遅延しています。	The processing of the <u>purchase request</u> form sent from the sales office is delayed by one month.

注文書（order）
請求書（invoice）
受領書（delivery report）
寄付金（donations）

展開文

	日本語	英語
1.1	営業所から回付された購買依頼書がまだ処理されていません。	The purchase request form sent from the sales office has not been processed yet.
1.2	営業所から回付された購買依頼書は何故処理されていないのでしょうか？	Why hasn't the purchase request form sent from the sales office been processed?
1.3	営業所から回付された購買依頼書は1か月前に処理されているはずでした。	The purchase request form sent from the sales office should have been processed one month ago.
1.4	営業所に問い合わせて必要な対応をして下さい。	Please contact the sales office and take necessary steps.
1.5	営業所からようやく購買依頼書が提出されたので，早急に処理しました。	The purchase request form was finally sent from the sales office, so we processed it immediately.

Case 77 値引等の承認エビデンスがないことを指摘する

基本文

	日本語	英 語
2	<u>値引</u>を承認するためのエビデンスがありません。	There is no back-up to approve the <u>**discount**</u>.

返品（sales return）
リベート（rebate）
仕入割引（purchase discount）
販売手数料（sales commission）
関税（customs duty）
還付金（refund）
クレジット・メモ（credit memo）

展開文

	日本語	英 語
2.1	値引を承認するためのエビデンスはどれでしょうか？	What is the back-up to approve the discount?
2.2	値引を承認するためのエビデンスを送って下さい。	Send us the back-up to approve the discount.
2.3	値引を承認するためのエビデンスを入手するべきでした。	The back-up to approve the discount should have been obtained.
2.4	値引を承認するためのエビデンスは保管するようにして下さい。	The back-up to approve the discount should be stored.
2.5	値引を行う時は，必ず覚書を交わすようにして下さい。	Memorandums should be exchanged when discounts are approved.

Case 78　検収登録されていない資産について指摘する

基本文

	日本語	英 語
3	<u>資産Bの検収</u>がシステム上登録されていません。	The <u>acceptance of Asset B</u> has not been recorded in the system.

得意先（client）
仕入先（vendor）
固定資産（fixed asset）
単価（unit price）
仕入先コード（vendor's code）
法定耐用年数（statutory useful life）
取引日レート（spot rate）
減価償却累計額（accumulated depreciation expense）
陳腐化した棚卸資産（obsolete inventory）

展開文

	日本語	英 語
3.1	システム上検収登録されていない資産があります。	There is an asset not recorded in the system as accepted yet.
3.2	システム上，資産Bが検収登録されていないのは何故でしょうか？	Why isn't the acceptance of Asset B recorded in the system?
3.3	資産Bは1週間前に検収登録されるべきでした。	The acceptance of Asset B should have been recorded in the system one week ago.
3.4	購買担当者に連絡し，至急登録して下さい。	Contact the purchasing division staff, and process the acceptance immediately.
3.5	直ちに原因を調査し，報告して下さい。	Please investigate the cause and report to us without delay.

Case 79 注文書等の紛失について連絡する

基本文

	日本語	英語
4	申し訳ありません。<u>注文書</u>は購買担当者が紛失したそうです。	Sincere appologies. It appears that the purchasing division staff mislaid the <u>order form</u>.

受領書（delivery report）
注文請書（confirmation of order）
見積書（quotation）
検収書（acceptance report）
契約書（contract）

展開文

	日本語	英語
4.1	申し訳ありません。購買担当者が注文書をなくしたと聞きました。	Sincere appologies. I heard that the purchasing division staff mislaid the order form.
4.2	申し訳ありません。購買担当者によるミスで注文書を紛失したそうです。	Sincere appologies. It appears that order form was mislaid due by the purchasing division staff.
4.3	申し訳ありません。購買部の注文書の管理に不備があったようです。	Sincere appologies. It appears that there were deficiencies in the purchasing division in handling the order form.
4.4	今後注文書が紛失されないように保管方法を見直して頂けますか。	Please reassess how order forms are stored, so they will not be misplaced in the future.
4.5	保管方法については購買部門内で共有するようにして下さい。	The storage method should be communicated within the purchasing division.

Case 80　納品期限等の遅れに対するベンダーへのクレーム

基本文

	日本語	英　語
5	<u>納品期限</u>が守られていないようですので，ベンダーGに確認致します。	I will confirm with Vendor G why the <u>delivery deadline</u> has not been met.

数量（quantity）
品質（quality）
送付方法（delivery method）
支払期限（payment deadline）
仕様（specification）

展開文

	日本語	英　語
5.1	ベンダーGの納品期限が遅れがちですので，確認致します。	I will confirm why Vendor G's deliveries have a tendency to be late.
5.2	納品期限の遅延について，ベンダーGに確認致します。	I will confirm with Vendor G why the deliveries are delayed.
5.3	納品期限が今後守られるよう，ベンダーGと確認致します。	I will ask Vendor G to ensure future delivery deadlines are met.
5.4	ベンダーGの担当者は改善すると言っていましたが，引き続き注意が必要です。	Vendor G said that the situation will be improved, but we will to keep an eye on this.
5.5	他のベンダーの選定を検討致します。	We will consider choosing another vendor.

3　子会社，取引先等へのクレーム・対応

3　入出金に関するクレーム・対応

Case 81　売掛金等の回収遅延について対応を依頼する

基本文

	日本語	英　語
1	A社から<u>売掛金</u>が回収できていないようですので，至急対応して下さい。	It appears that <u>trade receivables</u> have not been collected from Company A, so please take immediate action.

受取手形（notes receivable）
貸付金（loan receivable）
未収入金（other account receivable）
立替費用（reimburse for expenses）
違約金（penalty charges）

展開文

	日本語	英　語
1.1	A社から先月の売掛金が回収できていないようですので，優先して対応してもらえますか。	It appears that last month's trade receivables have not been collected from Company A. Could you please deal with this as a priority?
1.2	A社から売掛金が回収できていない理由を至急確認して下さい。	Please confirm why trade receivables have not been collected from Company A.
1.3	A社からの売掛金は15日に回収が予定されていました。	Trade receivables should have been collected from Company A on the 15th.
1.4	A社から先月の売掛金が回収できていないようです。A社の資産に担保を設定することはできませんか？	It appears that last month's trade receivables have not been collected from Company A. Can we take out a mortgage on the Company A's assets?
1.5	売掛金が具体的にいつ回収できるのか，早急に確認して下さい。必要であれば貸倒引当金の計上を検討して下さい。	Please confirm when exactly the trade receivables will be collected as soon as possible. Please consider providing a bad debt reserve, if necessary.

Case 82　請求書等と出金額の不一致について指摘する

基本文

	日本語	英　語
2	<u>請求書</u>と出金額が一致しませんので，調査して頂けますか。	**Could you please investigate why the paid amount does not agree with the invoice?**

注文書（purchase order）
納品書（delivery report）
買掛金明細（detail report of trade payable）
支払手形明細（detail report of notes payable）
基本請負契約書（master services agreement）

展開文

	日本語	英　語
2.1	請求書と出金額とが10,000円ずれていますので，調査して下さい。	There is a JPY10,000 difference between the invoice and the paid amount. Could you please look into this?
2.2	請求書と出金額が異なる理由について教えて下さい。	Please tell me why the paid amount does not agree with the invoice.
2.3	請求書と出金額は一致するはずです。	The paid amount should agree with the invoice.
2.4	出金前に請求書の記載内容に注意するようにして下さい。	Please pay attention to the description in the invoice before making the payment.
2.5	請求額が変更になった場合，請求書は再発行される必要があります。	The invoice should be reissued if the billing amount has been changed.

Case 83　経費等の支払催促に対する対応を依頼する

基本文

	日本語	英　語
3	<u>税理士報酬</u>の支払催促がきていますので，早急に支払って下さい。	Please pay the <u>tax accountant's fee</u>, as we are receiving demands for payment.

監査報酬（audit fee）
弁護士報酬（attorney's fee）
業務委託料（outsourcing expense）
システム使用料（IT expense）
会社設立に関するコスト（incorporation cost）

展開文

	日本語	英　語
3.1	税理士報酬がまだ支払われていないようですので，早急に支払って頂けますか。	Please pay the tax accountant's fee as soon as possible, as it appears that it has not been paid yet.
3.2	税理士事務所から支払いを催促されております。早急に対処して頂けますか。	We are receiving demands for payment of the tax accountant's fee. Please make payment as soon as possible.
3.3	税理士報酬の支払期限は先月の30日でした。	The due date for paying the tax accountant's fee was the 30th of last month.
3.4	先月の税理士報酬はいくらでしたでしょうか。支払期日には残高が十分にあることを確認して頂けますか。	How much did you pay to the tax accountant last month? Please make sure that there are sufficient funds on the due date for payment.
3.5	請求書の支払期日は必ず確認するようにして下さい。	Please make sure to check the invoices for the payment due date.

Case 84　入金遅延への対応を依頼する

基本文

	日本語	英　語
4	<u>入金遅延</u>について2月10日に連絡しましたが，まだ返事を頂いていません。	We contacted you regarding the <u>delayed payment</u> on February 10, but we have not heard from you yet.

会計処理の遅延（delayed journal entry）
見積り（quotation）
商品発送（product shipping）
注文（order）
融資限度額（line of credit）
未収配当金（dividend receivable）

展開文

	日本語	英　語
4.1	入金遅延について1週間前に連絡しましたが，ご連絡を頂けますか。	We contacted you regarding the delayed payment a week ago. Could you please contact us?
4.2	2月10日に連絡した入金遅延の件はどうなっているか説明して頂けますでしょうか。	Please provide an explanation regarding the delayed payment we contacted you about on February 10.
4.3	入金遅延の件について，明日17:00までに返事を下さい。	Please contact us regarding the delayed payment by 17:00 tomorrow.
4.4	月次決算の関係もありますので，早めに連絡をするようにして下さい。	Please provide early notice, as we must complete the monthly closing.
4.5	入金が早急に行われるよう，催促して下さい。	Please make payment requests so that the payment will be made shortly.

Case 85　出金規定等の社内ルールの再検討を依頼する

基本文

	日本語	英語
5	<u>出金</u>の承認規程について，見直しが必要です。	It is necessary to reconsider the approval guideline of <u>cash disbursements</u>.

入金（cash receipts）
重要な資本的支出（significant capital expenditures）
海外送金（outbound money transfer）
返金（refund）
現金同等物（cash equivalents）
買戻し契約（repurchase agreement）
外部取引（external transactions）
器具備品の取得（addition of furniture and fixtures）
顧客の債務不履行（customer's default）

展開文

	日本語	英語
5.1	出金の社内ルールについて再検討致します。	We will reconsider the internal rules on cash disbursements.
5.2	出金の承認者について見直しを行います。	We will reconsider who should approve the cash disbursements.
5.3	出金の承認規程は来月末までに見直します。	We will review and update the approval guidelines for cash disbursements by the end of next month.
5.4	承認者以外にチェック担当者を置くことを検討します。	We will consider having it reviewed by someone other than the approver.
5.5	出金金額によって，必要な承認者を変更するようにします。	We will have different levels of approvals, depending on the amount of payment.

4 人件費(その他)に関するクレーム・対応

Case 86　時間外労働の承認が確認できないことを指摘する

基本文

	日本語	英語
1	<u>時間外労働</u>の承認が確認できません。	We cannot confirm the approval of <u>overtime</u>.

給与（payroll）
退職金（retirement allowance）
賞与引当金（accrued bonus）
退職給付引当金（accrued pension cost）
時間給労働者への給与（payroll for part-timers）

展開文

	日本語	英語
1.1	時間外労働の承認者のサインがありません。	The signature of the approver of overtime is missing.
1.2	時間外労働の承認が人事部マネージャーのものではありません。	Overtime was not approved by the Human Resource Division manager.
1.3	時間外労働の承認を確認できるようにして頂けますか。	Could you make sure that the approval of overtime can be confirmed?
1.4	適切な権限者の承認があることを確認するようにして下さい。	Ensure that it has been approved by someone with appropriate authority.
1.5	時間外労働の承認が承認日以降となっているので，今後は事前に取るように徹底して下さい。	You obtained the overtime approval after the day when the overtime hours were recorded. Please make sure to obtain an approval beforehand in the future.

Case 87　給与等の支払超過への対応を依頼する

基本文

	日本語	英　語
2	<u>給与</u>の支払超過は翌月の支払金額で調整して下さい。	**The overpayment of <u>payroll</u> should be adjusted in next month's payment amount.**

賞与（bonus）
所得税（income tax）
州税（state tax）
社会保険料（social security expense）
派遣社員の給与（payroll for temporary workers）

展開文

	日本語	英　語
2.1	給与の支払超過は翌月の支払金額から減額して下さい。	The overpayment of payroll should be deducted from next month's payment amount.
2.2	給与の支払超過は，6月の支払金額で調整して下さい。	The overpayment of payroll should be adjusted in the payment amount for June.
2.3	給与の支払超過があった場合は，翌月の支払金額で調整するようにして下さい。	If an overpayment of payroll occurs, it should be adjusted in next month's payment amount.
2.4	給与計算は非常に重要ですので，正確に行うようにして下さい。	Please ensure that payroll is accurately calculated, as it is important.
2.5	給与計算は必ずマネージャーのレビューを受けるようにして下さい。	The payroll calculation must be reviewed by the manager.

Case 88　依頼資料の送付を督促する

基本文

	日本語	英　語
3	前に依頼した<u>不動産鑑定評価書</u>を至急送付して下さい。	Please immediately send us the <u>real estate appraisal report</u> we requested previously.

有価証券時価情報（market price information of security）
デューデリジェンスレポート（due diligence report）
無形資産の評価レポート（valuation report of intangible asset）
ミーティング・アジェンダ（meeting agenda）
財務制限条項（financial covenant）
目論見書（offering circular）
自己株式の調整表（reconciliation schedule of treasury stock）
日系企業向けのレポート（report for Japanese companies）

展開文

	日本語	英　語
3.1	前に依頼した不動産鑑定評価書はいつ送って頂けるのですか？	When will the real estate appraisal report we requested previously be sent?
3.2	先週依頼した不動産鑑定書を受領しておりません。	We haven't received the real estate appraisal report we requested last week.
3.3	前に依頼した不動産鑑定依頼書を金曜日までに送付して下さい。	Please send the real estate appraisal report we requested previously by Friday.
3.4	監査人から催促されていますので、早急に対応して下さい。	Please take care of it as soon as possible, as we are being pressed by our auditors.
3.5	取り急ぎ、不動産鑑定評価書をファックスで送付して下さい。	Please fax us the real estate appraisal report for now.

Case 89　重大なクレーム等の連絡を依頼する

基本文

	日本語	英　語
4	<u>重大なクレーム</u>があった場合に適時に連絡して頂けますか。	<u>Serious complaints</u> should be communicated on a timely basis.

係争事件（litigation）
不正行為（fraud）
重要な契約の締結（execution of significant contract）
重要な虚偽表示（material misstatement）
計算誤り（calculation error）

展開文

	日本語	英　語
4.1	重大なクレームがあった場合は遅滞なく連絡するようにして下さい。	Serious complaints should be communicated as soon as possible.
4.2	重大なクレームがあった場合はすぐに本社に連絡しなければなりません。	Serious complaints must be communicated to the Parent Company on a timely basis.
4.3	重大なクレームは速やかに報告されるべきでした。	Serious complaints should have been reported promptly.
4.4	弁護士と連携して，解決策を講じて下さい。見積コストについても報告して下さい。	Consult with your lawyer, and come up with a solution. Also, please report to us your estimated cost.
4.5	御社の監査役とも十分に協議して下さい。	Make sure to discuss thoroughly with your Corporate auditors.

Case 90　従業員等の処分について連絡する

基本文

	日本語	英語
5	不正を行った<u>従業員</u>の処分は，現在検討中です。	We are currently considering a penalty for the <u>employee</u> who committed an illegal act.

経営者（management）
取締役（executive director）
業務委託者（subcontractor）
監査役（corporate auditor）
執行役（executive officer）
元従業員（former employee）
監査委員会のメンバー（a member of audit committee）

展開文

	日本語	英語
5.1	不正を行った従業員の処分について，現在協議を行っております。	The penalty for the employee who committed an illegal act is currently under discussion.
5.2	不正を行った従業員の処分につきましては，もう少しお待ち頂けますか。	Could you please wait until the penalty for the employee who committed an illegal act is determined?
5.3	不正を行った従業員の処分は，今週末までに決定致します。	The penalty for the employee who committed an illegal act will be determined by the end of the week.
5.4	従業員の横領に対する再発防止策を提出して下さい。	Please submit the measures to prevent recurrence/reoccurrence of misappropriation by employees.
5.5	再発防止策は具体的に記載して下さい。	Measures to prevent recurrence/reoccurrence should be described in detail.

5　予算に関するクレーム・対応

Case 91　差異分析の誤りを指摘する

基本文

	日本語	英　語
1	<u>予算と実績の差異分析</u>が正しくありません。	The <u>analysis of the difference between budget and actual figures</u> is incorrect.

前期と当期の差異分析（analysis of difference between current year balance and prior year balance）
予算システムへの入力（input to budget system）
レポーティングパッケージの作成（input to reporting package）
売上分析（sales analysis）
（実地棚卸の）数量差異分析（analysis of quantity variance）

展開文

	日本語	英　語
1.1	予算と実績の差異分析項目に漏れが多数あります。	There are many omissions in the analysis of the difference between budget and actual amounts.
1.2	予算と実績の差異分析に誤りが散見されます。	There are errors in various parts of the analysis of the difference between budget and actual amounts.
1.3	予算実績分析は前にお送りしたマニュアルに沿って行うべきでした。	The budget-actual analysis should have been performed according to the manual we sent previously.
1.4	差異が100万円以上ある全ての項目について，原因を説明して下さい。	All items whose differences exceed JPY 1 million should be explained.
1.5	分析の内容が非常に全般的なものに見受けられます。より詳細な内容に修正して下さい。	It appears that only general explanations are given. Please amend to provide more detailed explanations.

Case 92　入力漏れ・エラーについて指摘する

基本文

	日本語	英　語
2	<u>入力が漏れている箇所</u>があるため，エラーが発生しています。	An error was detected, as there were <u>missing fields</u>.

入力ミス（typing error）
環境依存文字（environment dependent characters）
値の範囲を超えた数値（amounts over limit）

展開文

	日本語	英　語
2.1	エラーが発生していますので，至急入力が漏れている箇所に記入して下さい。	Please fill in the blanks immediately, as an error was detected.
2.2	PL項目の記入に漏れがありますので，エラーメッセージが出ています。	An error message was displayed because certain income statement items were not filled out.
2.3	入力されていない箇所があると，エラーが表示されるようになっています。	It is designed so that an error message will be displayed when there are missing fields.
2.4	今後エラーが発生している時は，入力を見直すようにしてもらえますか。	From now on, could you check the input when an error is detected?
2.5	資料を提出する前に，全てのエラーが解消されたことを確認することを徹底して下さい。	You must make sure that all errors have been resolved before submitting the document.

Case 93　交際費等，費用の大幅増加について指摘する

基本文

	日本語	英　語
3	交際費の実績が予算に比べて多い理由を説明して下さい。	Please explain why the actual amount of <u>entertainment fees</u> exceeded the budget.

福利厚生費（welfare expense）
旅費交通費（travel expense）
会議費（meeting expense）
広告宣伝費（advertisement cost）
オペレーティング・リース費用（operating lease expense）
勤務費用（service cost）
株式報酬費用（share-based compensation）

展開文

	日本語	英　語
3.1	予算額の2倍の交際費が支出された理由は何でしょうか。	Why was twice the amount of budgeted entertainment fees expensed?
3.2	交際費の予算と実績の差額について詳しく教えて下さい。	Please explain in detail the difference between the budgeted and actual amount of entertainment fees.
3.3	交際費の実績が予算をこれほど上回ることは想定されていませんでした。来年度の費用となる交際費が実績に含まれているのではないですか？	We did not expect the actual amount of entertainment fees to exceed the budget by so much. Did you include any entertainment fees which will be incurred in the following year?
3.4	不自然に変動している勘定科目には注意するようにして頂けますか。	Please watch out for accounts with unusual fluctuations.
3.5	従業員不正が疑われますので，至急調査して下さい。	Please investigate immediately, as an illegal act by the employee is suspected.

Case 94　上長の承認漏れについて指摘する

基本文

	日本語	英　語
4	お送り頂いた資料に，<u>CFO</u>の承認がありません。	The submitted document was not approved by the <u>CFO</u>.

社長（CEO）
取締役（executive director）
本部長（general manager）
課長（chief of department）

展開文

	日本語	英　語
4.1	お送り頂いた資料上で，CFOの承認の証跡を確認することができません。	We could not confirm that the submitted document was approved by the CFO.
4.2	お送り頂いた資料ですが，CFOの承認が漏れているようです。	It appears that the CFO's approval is missing on the submitted document.
4.3	お送り頂いた資料は，CFOが承認する必要があります。	The submitted document had to be approved by the CFO.
4.4	正式な承認が行われたかどうかわかりませんので，確認して下さい。	Please check, as we are not sure if it has been approved appropriately.
4.5	必要な承認権限について，必ず確認するようにして下さい。	Make sure to check the necessary authorization.

Case 95 クレームに対して謝罪する

基本文

	日本語	英　語
5	度重なるミス，大変申し訳ありません。<u>再発防止策</u>（の導入）を検討致します。	We are very sorry for the repeated mistakes. We will implement <u>measures to prevent them</u>.

チェック体制の見直し（reconsideration of reviewing policy）
業務マニュアルの改訂（revision of operation manual）
スタッフの再教育（re-education of staff）
担当者の交代（rotation of person in charge）
複雑な取引に関するプロセス（process for complicated transactions）

展開文

	日本語	英　語
5.1	ご不便をおかけし，大変申し訳ありません。今後このようなことがないように気をつけます。	We are very sorry for the inconvenience. We will make sure that this does not happen in the future.
5.2	多大なご迷惑をおかけして申し訳ありません。以後気をつけます。	We apologize for the inconvenience. We will be careful from now on.
5.3	度重なる失礼，大変申し訳ありません。もっと気をつけるべきでした。	We are very sorry for the inconvenience. We should have been more careful.
5.4	作業分担を再検討致します。	We will reconsider the allocation of work.
5.5	担当者を教育し，スキルアップに務めます。	We will educate the staff in charge and improve their skills.

6　決算に関するクレーム・対応

Case 96　連結パッケージの提出遅延について指摘する

基本文

	日本語	英語
1	提出期限が過ぎておりますが，連結パッケージをまだ受領できておりません。	We haven't received the reporting package yet, even though the due date has passed.

試算表（trial balance）　法定監査の監査報告書（audit report of statutory audit）
貸借対照表（balance sheet）　キャッシュフロー計算書（cash flow statement）
損益計算書（income statement）　開示資料（supporting documents for disclosure）
予算（budget）　管理会計用のレポート（report for management accounting）

展開文

	日本語	英語
1.1	連結パッケージの提出期限は2月10日でしたが，まだ受領できておりません。	The due date for submitting the reporting package was February 10, but we haven't received it yet.
1.2	連結パッケージの提出期限は3日前でしたが，まだ受領できておりません。	The due date for submitting the reporting package was three days ago, but we haven't received it yet.
1.3	連結パッケージの提出期限は先日メールで連絡したとおりです。	We have informed you of the deadline for submitting the reporting package by email the other day.
1.4	連結パッケージはいつ頃送って頂けますでしょうか。	Please inform us when the reporting package will be submitted.
1.5	スケジュール通りに決算報告が行われなくなる恐れがありますので，早急に連結パッケージを送って頂けますでしょうか。	Please submit the reporting package immediately. Otherwise, we cannot meet the deadline of financial closing schedule.

Case 97　会計基準からの逸脱を指摘する

基本文

	日本語	英　語
2	決算マニュアルに準拠していない会計処理があります。	There is an accounting treatment not in accordance with the <u>accounting manual</u>.

国際財務報告基準（IFRS）
米国会計基準（US-GAAP）
グループ会計ポリシー（group accounting policy）
親会社の会計方針（parent company accounting policy）
新会計基準（newly adopted accounting policy）
定額法（straight-line method）
定率法（declining balance method）
先入先出法（first-in first-out method）
定価法（lower of cost or market method）
移動平均法（moving average method）
総平均法（weighted-average method）
工事進行基準（percentage of completion method）

展開文

	日本語	英　語
2.1	収益認識の会計処理は決算マニュアルに準拠していません。	Revenue recognition is not in accordance with the accounting manual.
2.2	収益認識の会計処理は決算マニュアルに記載されたとおりです。	The accounting treatment for revenue recognition is described in the accounting manual.
2.3	収益認識は決算マニュアルに準拠して処理するべきでした。	The transaction should have been treated in accordance with revenue recognition criteria in the accounting manual.
2.4	収益認識の会計処理を決算マニュアルに合わせて下さい。	Please correct the revenue recognition according to the accounting manual.
2.5	期末日時点で未検収の商品にかかる収益を修正して下さい。	Please correct the revenue recognized for unaccepted goods at year-end.

Case 98 会計方針の変更の事前連絡を依頼する

基本文

	日本語	英　語
3	<u>会計方針</u>の変更につきましては，事前に本社経理と協議するようにして下さい。	If you intend to change the <u>accounting policy</u>, please consult the parent company's accounting department prior to closing.

勘定科目区分（account classification）
表示方法（disclosure policy）
会計ソフトウェア（accounting software）
別掲項目（separate line item）
会計上の見積り（accounting estimate）

展開文

	日本語	英　語
3.1	会計方針を変える時は，事前に本社経理と協議するようにして頂けますか。	If you are changing the accounting policy, could you please consult with the parent company's accounting department prior to closing?
3.2	事前に本社経理と協議してから，会計方針を変更するようにして下さい。	Please change you accounting policy after consulting with the parent company's accounting department prior to closing.
3.3	会計方針の変更は，事前に本社経理と協議するべきでした。	If you intended to change the accounting policy, the parent company's accounting department should have been consulted prior to closing.
3.4	会計方針の変更については独自に判断しないで下さい。	If you intend to change the accounting policy, please do not make decisions on your own.
3.5	会計方針に関しては，日頃から本社経理とコミュニケーションを取るようにして下さい。	Please communicate with the parent company's accounting department regularly regarding accounting policy.

Case 99　決算スケジュールの徹底を依頼する

基本文

	日本語	英　語
4	<u>決算スケジュール</u>について社内で周知し徹底するようにして下さい。	Please keep the employees of your Company informed about the <u>closing schedule</u>.

月次決算スケジュール（monthly closing schedule）
四半期決算スケジュール（quarterly closing schedule）
報告書日（reporting date）
研修日程（training schedule）
期末監査スケジュール（year-end audit schedule）
収益認識の新しいガイダンスの適用（adoption of new revenue recognition guidance）

展開文

	日本語	英　語
4.1	社内において，決算スケジュールの周知を徹底して下さい。	The closing schedule should be well communicated within your Company.
4.2	決算スケジュールは全ての社員に周知徹底するようにして頂けますか。	Could you ensure all employees are informed about the closing schedule?
4.3	決算スケジュールについて社内で周知徹底するようにすべきでした。	The employees of your Company should have been well informed about the closing schedule.
4.4	決算スケジュールは，経理担当者が責任を持って周知して下さい。	The Accounting staff is responsible for informing employees about the closing schedule.
4.5	今後このようなことがないように，決算スケジュールの伝達は徹底して下さい。	Please make sure to inform employees about the closing schedule so that this does not happen in the future.

Case 100　他部門との連携を強化する

基本文

	日本語	英 語
5	<u>経理部門以外の部門</u>から，資料が迅速に提出されるようにします。	We will cooperate with staff from <u>departments other than accounting</u>, so that documents are submitted promptly.

工場（factory）
支店（branch）
営業所（business office）
関連会社（affiliated company）
100％子会社（wholly-owned subsidiary）

展開文

	日本語	英 語
5.1	資料が迅速に提出されるよう，経理部門以外の部門と協力します。	We will ensure the prompt submission of documents by cooperating with the staff of departments other than accounting.
5.2	経理部門以外の部門からも，資料が迅速に提出されるように努力します。	We will make efforts so that documents would be submitted promptly from departments other than accounting too.
5.3	経理部門以外の部門から，資料が迅速に提出されるようにするべきでした。	We should have cooperated with staff of departments other than accounting, so that documents are submitted promptly.
5.4	経理部門以外の部門の担当者に，資料の重要性について説明します。	We will explain the importance of the documents to the staff of other departments.
5.5	経理部門以外の部門の担当者と，資料の管理方法について相談します。	We will discuss the management of the documents with the staff of other departments.

3　子会社，取引先等へのクレーム・対応

7　内部統制に関するクレーム・対応

Case 101　職務分掌上の問題点を指摘する

基本文

	日本語	英　語
1	<u>経理部門</u>の職務分掌が適切に行われていません。	The segregation of duties in the <u>accounting department</u> seems to be inappropriate.

営業部門（sales department）
人事部門（human resource department）
IT部門（IT department）
製造部門（manufacturing department）

展開文

	日本語	英　語
1.1	経理部門において職務分掌が十分に行われているのでしょうか？	Are the preparer and the approver in the accounting department segregated properly?
1.2	経理部門において，作成者と承認者が区分されていません。	The preparer and the approver in the accounting department are not properly segregated.
1.3	今後，経理部門の職務分掌を適切に行うよう，徹底して下さい。	Please make sure that the appropriate accounting segregation of duties is in place from now on.
1.4	販売システムの入力者と承認者を明確にして下さい。	Please clarify who inputs information in the sales system and who approves it.
1.5	売上伝票が起票者と承認者によって必ずサインされるように徹底して下さい。	You must make sure that the sales vouchers are signed by both the preparer and approver.

Case 102 統制テスト手法の相違を指摘する

基本文

	日本語	英 語
2	<u>テスト件数</u>がガイドラインと異なります。	The <u>number of samples</u> tested does not agree with the guidelines.

テスト方法（testing method）
サンプリング方法（sampling method）
アップデート手続（roll-forward procedure）

展開文

	日本語	英 語
2.1	実際にテストされた件数と，ガイドラインに示されたテスト件数が異なります。	The number of samples tested is different from the number of samples indicated in the guidelines.
2.2	テストされた件数は15件ですが，ガイドラインに示されたテスト件数は25件です。	15 samples were tested, but the number of samples indicated in the guidelines is 25.
2.3	テスト件数はガイドラインに示されているとおりです。	The number of samples to test is indicated in the guidelines.
2.4	ガイドラインは事前に注意して読むようにして下さい。	The guidelines should be read carefully prior to the testing.
2.5	早急に追加テストを行い，結果を報告して下さい。	Additional testing should be performed, and the results should be reported as soon as possible.

Case 103 証憑の未提出を指摘する

基本文

	日本語	英　語
3	<u>在庫の検収</u>に関する証憑がありません。	Evidence of the <u>acceptance of inventory</u> is missing.

売上の認識（revenue recognition）
給与の支払（payroll payment）
固定資産購入（purchase of fixed asset）
借入契約（loan agreement）
議決権（voting rights）
延滞金（delinquent charge）
偶発債務（contingent liabilities）
繰延費用（deferred costs）
永久差異（permanent differences）
免税取引（tax exempt transaction）
非課税取引（non-taxable transaction）

展開文

	日本語	英　語
3.1	提出された書類の中から，在庫の検収に関する証憑が見つかりませんでした。	We couldn't find the evidence for the acceptance of inventory in the submitted documents.
3.2	在庫の検収に関する証憑がないようですので確認して下さい。	We can't find the evidence for the acceptance of inventory. Please check.
3.3	在庫の検収に関する証憑の提出が求められていました。	The submission of the evidence for the acceptance of inventory was required.
3.4	在庫の検収に関する証跡は必ず保管するようにして頂けますか。	Please make sure that the evidence related to the receipt and inspection of inventory is preserved.
3.5	書類を提出する前に，内容を注意深くチェックするようにしてもらえますか。	Could you check your documents carefully before submitting them?

Case 104 統制の不備是正への対応を依頼する

基本文

	日本語	英語
4	<u>不備が検出されたコントロールNo.1の是正措置</u>について早急に連絡して下さい。	**Please contact us immediately on the remedial actions of Control No.1, where a deficiency was detected.**

統制不備要約表（summary of control deficiencies）
全社統制チェックリスト（entity level control checklist）
進捗管理表（time schedule sheet）

展開文

	日本語	英語
4.1	報告期限が過ぎていますので、コントロールNo.1の是正措置について早急に連絡してもらえますか。	Could you contact us immediately on the remedial actions of Control No.1, as the due date has already passed?
4.2	提出書類にコントロールNo.1の是正措置が記載されていませんでしたので、早急に連絡して下さい。	Please contact us immediately on the remedial actions of Control No.1, as it was not described in the submitted document.
4.3	不備の検出されたコントロールの是正措置は、5月31日までに報告することになっていました。	Remedial actions for control deficiencies should have been reported by May 31.
4.4	期末日まで期間がありませんので、早急に対応して下さい。	Please resolve it immediately, as there isn't much time before year-end.
4.5	是正された統制の再テストがまだ行われていないようでしたら、至急実施して下さい。	If the remediated controls have not been retested yet, please perform the testing as soon as possible.

3 子会社，取引先等へのクレーム・対応

Case 105　テスト証憑の準備について連絡する

基本文

	日本語	英語
5	<u>請求書</u>は早めに倉庫から取り寄せるように致します。	We will arrange to have the <u>invoices</u> sent from the warehouse earlier.

受領書（delivery report）
船荷証券（bill of lading）
仕掛品残高（balance of work in progress）
評価レポート（valuation report）

展開文

	日本語	英語
5.1	請求書は決算に間に合うように倉庫から取り寄せるように致します。	We will arrange to have the invoices sent from the warehouse in time for the closing.
5.2	請求書は3月までに倉庫から送ってもらうように致します。	We will have the invoices sent from the warehouse by March.
5.3	請求書は早めに倉庫から取り寄せるようにするべきでした。	We should have arranged to have the invoices sent from the warehouse earlier.
5.4	請求書を早めに出して頂けるように物流部門担当者と交渉します。	I will negotiate with the logistics department staff so that the invoices can be received earlier.
5.5	請求書の保管方法について見直したいと思います。	We would like to reassess the storage method for the invoices.

INDEX　＊本文にある用語には頁を記載

英・数字

1日前
one day earlier　*92*

1週間早く
one week earlier　*92*

5営業日前
5 business days earlier　*92*

9月30日に終了する9か月間の
for nine months period ended September 30　*94*

100％子会社
wholly-owned subsidiary　*173*

100万円未満の修正
revising entries smaller than JPY 1 million　*101*

A社からの入金
payment from A company　*111*

CFO（最高財務責任者）
CFO　*38, 127, 167*

IT全般統制
IT general controls　*106*

IT全般統制の不備
deficiencies in IT general control　*139*

IT統制のテスト
test of IT application controls　*103*

IT部門
IT department　*174*

あ

相見積り
competitive quotes　*78*

アジェンダ（議題）
agenda　*33, 161*

値の範囲を超えた数値
amounts over limit　*165*

アップデートテスト
update testing　*103*

アップデート手続
roll-forward procedure　*175*

粗利益
gross profit　*72*

い

以後
from now on　*168*

委譲する
delegate　*23*

委託販売契約書
Consignment Sales Agreement　*10*

一括払い
lump-sum payment　*85*

一致する
agree with　*131*

一般管理費
general expenses　*137*

移転価格
transfer pricing　*115*

移転価格税制
transfer pricing taxation　*20*

移転価格税制に関する事前確認（APA）
the Advance Pricing Agreement（APA）　*125*

異動
personnel transfer　*12*

移動平均法
moving average method　*170*

委任契約書
Delegation Agreement　*10*

委任状
Power of Attorney　*11*

違約金
penalty charges　*84, 154*

入れ替え
replacement　*81*

う

ウォークスルー
walkthrough　*103*
ウォークスルー資料
walk-through documents　*102*
請負契約書
Service Agreement　*10*
受取手形
notes receivable　*148, 154*
受取手数料
commission fee
受取人
payee　*86*
受取配当金
dividend income
受取利息
interest income　*130*
受取ロイヤリティー
royalty income
内訳
breakdown　*67, 68, 72, 121, 137*
売上計上
posting of sales　*111*
売上原価
cost of sales　*87, 130*
売上債権
receivables　*20*
売上仕訳入力
inputting of sales journal entries　*107*
売上総利益
gross profit　*72*
売上総利益率
GP ratio　*72*
売上高
sales figures　*72*
売上帳
sales subledger　*147*

売上伝票
sales voucher　*145, 174*
売上取引
sales transactions　*110*
売上の認識
revenue recognition　*176*
売上プロセス
sales process　*102*
売上分析
sales analysis　*164*
売上予算
sales budget　*96*
売上予算のセグメント別
sales budget by segment　*93*
売上割引関連証憑
evidence relating to sales discounts　*76*
売掛金
trade receivables　*154*
accounts receivable（AR）
売掛金回収期間
trade receivable collection deadline　*146*
売掛金回転率
AR turnover ratio　*13*
売掛金残高
AR balance　*108*
売掛金残高明細
detail report of Trade Receivables　*148*
売掛金年齢表
AR aging list　*99*
売掛金の回収
AR collection　*13*
売掛金補助簿
trade receivable subledger　*147*
売掛金明細
an AR balance breakdown
運送費
transportation expense

運転資金
    working capital　*95*
運転資金残高
    working capital balance　*121*

え

永久差異
    permanent differences　*176*
営業外収益（費用）
    non-operating income（expense）
営業活動によるキャッシュ・フロー
    net cash provided by（used in） operating activities
営業時間
    business hours　*56*
    office hours　*12*
営業収入（損失）
    operating income（expense）
営業所
    business office　*173*
    sales office　*149*
営業成績
    operating results　*21, 130*
営業セグメント別売上
    sales by operating segment　*72*
営業担当者
    sales representative　*85*
営業日
    business days　*88*
営業部，営業部門
    sales department　*38, 174*
営業部門担当者
    sales division staff　*145*
役務収益
    service revenue　*72*
役務提供
    service rendered　*110*
エラーチェック機能
    error check function　*141*

エラーメッセージ
    error messages　*108*
延滞金
    delinquent charge　*176*
延長する
    extend　*86*
円安の影響
    impact by depreciation of yen　*119*

お

横領
    misappropriation　*163*
大口の新規顧客を獲得する
    win large new customers　*129*
遅れている
    be behind schedule　*111, 126, 146*
遅れる
    delayed　*146*
遅くとも
    at the latest　*111*
    latest　*76*
オフィス用家具
    office furniture　*79*
オペレーティング・リース
    operating lease　*166*
覚書
    Memorandum of Understanding　*11*
    memorandums　*150*
親会社株式
    shares of parent
親会社の会計方針
    parent company accounting policy　*170*

か

海外子会社
    foreign subsidiaries　*21*
海外出張
    be on business trip abroad　*50*
    overseas business trip　*49*

海外送金
　outbound money transfer　85, 158
外貨換算
　foreign currency translation
買掛金残高
　AP balance　113
買掛金残高明細
　AP breakdown　112
　detail report of trade payable　148
買掛金の年齢表
　AP aging list　112
買掛金補助簿
　trade payable subledger　147
買掛金明細
　detail report of trade payable　155
外貨建取引
　foreign currency transactions　20
外貨持出し制限
　the remittance limit on certain currencies　118
会議
　conference　28, 57
会議招集
　meeting invitation　32, 33
会議費
　meeting expense　166
会計
　accounting　56, 57
会計基準
　accounting standards　33, 34
会計システム
　accounting system　42, 81, 141
会計事務所による財務デューデリジェンス
　the financial Due Diligence procedures by the accounting firm　126
会計上の見積り
　accounting estimate　171

会計処理
　accounting treatment　13, 24, 58, 67, 170
会計処理の遅延
　delayed journal entry　157
会計ソフトウェア
　accounting software　171
会計帳簿
　accounting book　148
会計年度
　the fiscal year　128
会計方針
　accounting policy　99, 171
会計方針の変更
　change in accounting　12
外国税額控除
　Foreign Tax Credit　115
開示作成業務
　preparation of presentations and disclosures of financial statements　20
開示資料
　supporting documents for disclosure　169
会社設立
　incorporation　156
会社パンフレット
　company brochure　78
会社予算
　company budget　96
回収可能額
　recoverable amount　95
回収可能性
　recoverability　59
回収する
　collect　154
回収不能債権
　non-recoverable loan
解消される
　be fixed　82

改善計画
  remediation plan *104*
改善策
  action plan *139*
改善する
  improve *153*
  remediate *139*
外注先の内部統制
  internal controls at subcontractors *139*
回転期間
  turnover period *112*
回転率
  turnover ratio *95*
ガイドライン
  guidelines *175*
開発費
  development cost *77*
外部倉庫
  third party warehouse's *135*
外部取引
  external transactions *158*
外部の調査
  external investigation *90*
買戻し契約
  repurchase agreement *158*
解約不能リース
  non-cancelable leases *97*
解約料
  cancellation fee *85*
架空取引
  fictitious transactions *105*
確認状
  confirmation *73*
学歴
  academic background *42*
加工費
  conversion cost *77*
過去勤務費用
  prior service cost *87*

貸方残高
  credit balance *116*
貸倒損失
  bad debt expense *130*
貸倒引当金
  allowance for doubtful accounts *136*
  bad debt reserve *154*
  in allowance for doubtful accounts *132*
貸倒引当金繰入（戻入）額
  provision (reversal) of allowance for doubtful accounts
貸付金
  loan receivable *20, 154*
加重平均資本コスト
  weighted average cost of capital (WACC) *98*
過剰在庫
  excess inventory *135*
過少資本税制
  Thin Capitalization Rules *115*
可処分所得
  disposal income
課税所得
  taxable income *131*
課長
  assistant manager *20, 38*
  chief of department *167*
課徴金の支払い可能性
  probability of fines *124*
合併契約書
  Merger Agreement *10*
カテゴリー別の見積一般管理費
  estimated general expense by category *93*
必ず
  mandatory *91*
株式譲渡契約
  Stock Purchase Agreement (SPA) *110*

INDEX

株式売買契約書
　Stock Purchase Agreement　*10*
株式発行費
　stock issuance costs
株式報酬費用
　share-based compensation　*166*
株主
　shareholders　*99*
株主資本
　shareholders' equity
上半期
　the 1st half　*128*
借入契約
　loan agreement　*176*
借り換えを予定している短期借入金
　short-term loans expected to be refinanced on a long-term basis　*121*
借方残高
　debit balance　*116*
仮勘定
　suspense account　*121*
為替
　foreign currencies　*100*
為替換算調整勘定
　foreign currency translation adjustment
為替差益（損）
　foreign currency exchange gain（loss）　*100*
為替予約
　forward exchange contracts
為替レート
　foreign currency rate　*75*
環境依存文字
　environment dependent characters　*165*
環境対策費
　environmental charges　*137*
環境対策引当金
　environmental provision　*136*

関係会社売掛金
　accounts receivable from subsidiaries and associates - trade
関係会社株式
　shares of subsidiaries and associates
関係会社債権債務一覧表
　list of intercompany receivables/payables　*99*
関係会社残高確認の差異分析
　intercompany balance variance analysis　*116*
関係会社残高差異調整
　reconciliation of intercompany balance confirmation variance　*111, 126*
関係会社整理損失引当金
　provision for loss on liquidation of subsidiaries and associates
監査
　audit　*126*
監査委員会
　audit committee　*163*
監査計画と対象範囲
　audit planning and scoping　*106*
監査手続
　audit procedure　*126*
監査人
　auditor　*57, 58, 121*
監査報告書
　audit report　*123*
監査報酬
　audit fee　*156*
監査役
　corporate auditor　*124, 163*
勘定科目
　account classification　*171*
関税
　customs duty　*150*
間接費
　indirect costs　*129*

監督官庁
　regulatory authorities　*118*
還付金
　refund　*150*
還付請求
　claim for refund　*89*
管理会計
　management accounting　*169*
関連会社
　affiliated company　*173*
関連する関係会社間取引
　relevant inter-company transactions　*108*
関連当事者一覧表
　list of related parties　*97*
関連当事者との取引
　related party transactions　*115*

き

機械
　machinery　*79*
企画
　proposal　*43*
期間帰属
　cut off　*112*
企業結合
　business combinations　*114*
企業再編
　reorganization　*127*
企業内弁護士
　in-house lawyer　*91*
企業買収
　M&A　*57*
器具備品
　furniture and fixtures　*158*
議決権
　voting rights　*176*
期限
　deadline　*40, 45, 47, 48, 51, 52, 58, 67, 92*
　due　*52*
　due date　*58*
期限通り
　in time　*51, 59*
期限内
　on time　*42, 93*
記載内容
　description　*155*
期日
　deadline　*51*
　due　*52*
　due date　*49, 84*
期首残高
　opening balance　*134*
技術提携契約
　Technical Collaboration Agreement　*127*
議事録
　minutes　*18, 58*
既存の
　exising　*98*
議題
　agenda　*32*
期待運用収益率
　expected rate of return　*136*
期中監査
　interim audit　*126*
気付事項
　your findings　*104*
寄付金
　donations　*149*
基本請負契約書
　Master Services Agreement　*73, 155*
基本給
　base salary　*87*
期末監査
　year-end audit　*172*
期末残高
　closing balance　*134*

期末日
　fiscal year end date　*135*
期末日レート
　closing rates　*100*
キャッシュフロー計算書
　cash flow statement　*169*
吸収合併
　merger　*22*
急なお知らせ
　short notice　*92*
給与
　payroll　*87, 88, 159, 160*
給与規定
　payroll policy　*87*
　the payroll policy　*122*
給与計算期間
　the payroll period　*122*
給与計算業者
　the payroll service provider　*122*
給与計算システム
　the payroll system　*122*
給与テーブル
　payroll table　*122*
給与の支払
　payroll payment　*176*
給与の支払日
　the payday　*122*
教育する
　educate　*168*
協議する
　consult　*171*
今日中に
　by the end of today　*92*
業績評価
　performance evaluation　*95*
業務委託者
　subcontractor　*163*
業務委託料
　outsourcing expense　*156*

業務監査
　operational audit　*126*
業務記述書
　business process description　*102, 138*
業務マニュアルの改訂
　revision of operation manual　*168*
共有する
　share　*90*
虚偽表示
　misstatement　*162*
銀行残高調整
　bank reconciliation　*117*
銀行手数料
　bank charges　*84*
金庫の現物確認
　physical inspection of a safe box　*135*
金銭消費貸借契約書
　Loan Agreement　*10*
勤務費用
　service cost　*166*
金融
　finance　*57*
金融機関コード
　ABA number／IBAN/Sort Code　*120*
金融資産（負債）
　financial assets（liabilities）　*136*
金融商品会計
　financial instruments accounting　*22, 24*
金利スワップ
　interest rate swaps

く

偶発債務
　contingent liabilities　*176*
偶発事象
　contingency　*124*
クーリエ
　courier　*73*

苦情
  complaints *146*
繰越欠損金
  net operating loss carry forwards *132*
繰延資産
  deferred assets
繰延収益
  deferred revenue *136*
繰延税金資産（負債）
  deferred tax assets (liabilities) *59, 67, 99, 132*
繰延税金資産の回収可能性の検討
  evaluation of the recoverability of deferred tax assets *135*
繰延費用
  deferred costs *176*
グループ会計ポリシー
  group accounting policy *67, 170*
グループ会計マニュアル
  group accounting manual *67*
グループ内取引
  intercompany transactions *11*
クレジット・メモ
  credit memo *150*
グローバル化
  globalization *37*

け

経営会議議事録
  management meeting minutes *110*
経営企画室
  Corporate Planning Department *21*
経営指導料
  management fee *117*
経営者
  management *163*
経営者評価
  management assessment *106*
経営陣
  management *41*

計算誤り
  calculation error *162*
計上区分
  classified *68*
経常利益
  income from continuing operation *130*
係争
  dispute *91*
係争事件
  litigation *162*
継続企業の前提
  entity's ability to continue as a going concern *135*
経費を減らす
  reduce expenses *129*
契約期間
  contract term *75*
契約書
  contract *66, 73, 152*
契約締結
  binding contracts *107*
経理システムへの入力
  entries to the accounting system *101*
経理担当者
  accounting personnel *65*
経理部
  accounting department *16, 21, 22, 23, 35, 38, 39, 49, 58, 60, 64, 66, 77, 101, 114*
経理部長
  controller *21*
  financial controller *38*
  manager of accounting department *22*
  accounting manager
経理部長承認
  approval by Accounting Manager *13*
経理部門
  accounting department *174*

187

経理部門のスキルアップ
　improvement of skills of staff in the accounting department　*140*
経理本部長
　general manager of the Accounting department　*38*
決済期日
　settlement date　*119*
決済条件
　payment terms　*74*
決済日
　settlement date　*86*
決算業務の標準化
　standardization of financial statement close process（FSCP）　*140*
決算仕訳
　closing entries　*97*
決算スケジュール
　closing schedule　*33, 54, 100, 172*
決算早期化
　accelerate financial closing　*32*
決算方針
　accounting closing policy　*27*
決算マニュアル
　accounting manual　*170*
月次決算
　monthly closing　*20, 22, 23, 41, 47, 100, 157*
月次決算スケジュール
　monthly closing schedule　*172*
月次統制
　monthly controls　*141*
月次報告
　monthly report　*111*
月末から5日経過後
　5th day from the month-end　*52*
懸念事項
　concerns　*65*
原因
　cause　*95, 151*

見解
　explanation　*124*
　opinion　*91*
原価管理システム
　cost management system　*81*
減額する
　deduct　*160*
原価計算
　cost accounting　*20, 21, 98*
原価計算システムの導入
　deployment of costing system　*140*
原価計算を担当
　an incharge of cost accounting　*23*
減価償却期間
　depreciation period　*80*
減価償却費
　depreciation cost　*87*
　depreciation expense　*96, 130*
減価償却方法
　depreciation method　*80*
減価償却累計額
　accumulated depreciation expense　*151*
研究開発費
　R&D expense　*130*
現金
　cash　*114*
現金出納帳
　cashbook　*117*
現金同等物
　cash equivalents　*158*
原告
　plaintiff　*91*
検査
　inspection　*108*
現在価値
　present value　*136*
現在までの
　to date　*94*

原材料
　raw material　*78, 79*
検査書
　inspection report　*116*
減資
　capital reduction　*127*
現時点では
　At this stage　*103*
検収
　acceptance　*151*
検収基準
　customers' acceptance basis　*65*
検収書
　acceptance certificate　*111*
　acceptance report　*152*
研修日程
　training schedule　*172*
検出された
　detected　*139*
減少している
　decreased　*132*
建設仮勘定
　construction in progress　*114*
減損損失
　impairment loss　*136*
減損の兆候を識別する
　identify indication of an impairment　*98*
現地GAAPベースの財務諸表
　local GAAP based financial statements　*97*
現地会計基準とIFRSの差異の調査
　investigation of differences between the local GAAP and IFRS　*125*
現地法定財務諸表の監査
　local statutory audit　*126*
権利放棄証書
　waiver　*121*

こ

交換用部品
　spare parts　*79, 149*
恒久的施設
　Permanent Establishment（PE）　*115*
広告宣伝費
　advertisement cost　*166*
広告宣伝費を減らす
　reduce advertising expenses　*129*
広告費予算
　budget for advertisement　*96*
口座
　account　*84*
交際費
　entertainment fees　*166*
交際費の損金算入の可能性
　deductibility of entertainment expenses for tax purposes　*124*
交際費を減らす
　reduce entertainment expenses　*129*
口座番号
　bank account number　*120*
口座引き落とし
　bank withdrawal　*117*
工事進行基準
　percentage of completion method　*170*
交渉
　negotiation　*49*
工場
　factory　*173*
交渉する
　negotiate　*178*
工場長
　plant manager　*20*
更新する
　updated　*108*
公正価値
　fair value　*136*

INDEX

189

購入する
　purchase　*58*
公認会計士
　CPA　*21*
購買
　purchase　*64, 114*
購買依頼書
　purchase request　*149*
購買依頼申請書
　purchase request form　*112*
購買関連証憑
　documents related to purchases　*77*
購買システム
　purchasing system　*81*
購買申請書
　purchase order　*80*
購買担当者
　purchasing division staff　*151, 152*
購買プロセス
　purchase process　*67, 105*
購買予算
　purchase budget　*96*
合弁会社設立契約書
　Joint Venture Agreement　*10*
合理性がない
　unreasonable　*124*
考慮する
　take into consideration　*115*
子会社
　subsidiary　*21, 127*
小切手台帳
　check register　*82*
顧客
　customer　*65, 67, 72, 91, 158*
顧客情報
　customer information　*108*
顧客の与信情報
　customer's credit information　*108*
国際財務報告基準
　IFRS　*23, 170*

国際送金
　international transfer　*83*
小口現金
　petty cash　*129*
固定資産
　fixed asset　*66, 114, 151*
　PPE（property, plant and equipment）　*20*
固定資産受払表
　list of addition/disposal of fixed assets　*99*
固定資産購入
　purchase of fixed asset　*176*
固定資産除去益（損）
　gain（loss）on disposal of fixed assets
固定資産台帳
　fixed assets register　*116*
固定資産の実地棚卸
　fixed assets count　*135*
固定資産の取得プロセスのテスト
　test of fix assets procurement process　*140*
固定資産売却益（損）
　gain（loss）on sale of fixed assets
固定費
　fixed costs　*93*
固定負債
　fixed liabilities
このEメールを受け取ったらすぐに
　upon receipt of this email　*92*
個別原価計算
　job costing　*81, 114*
個別財務諸表
　stand-alone financial statements　*74*
顧問税理士の見解
　opinion of your tax advisor　*124*
顧問弁護士
　legal adviser　*91*
　legal counsel

顧問弁護士の見解
    an opinion of legal counsel   *123*
雇用契約書
    Employment Agreement   *10*
根拠資料
    supporting documents   *110*
今後
    from now on   *165, 174*
    in the future   *93*
今週末
    end of this week   *144*

さ

サービス完了日
    service completion date   *146*
サービス内容
    nature of service   *75*
差異
    variance   *94*
再委託請負契約書
    Subcontractor Service Agreement   *10*
債権回収
    AR collection   *107*
債権債務消去仕訳
    entries to eliminate intercompany debts and credits   *134*
最高財務責任者
    CFO（Chief Financial officer）   *20, 38, 127, 167*
在庫管理
    Inventory management   *20, 22*
在庫管理システム
    inventory management system   *81*
在庫の検収
    acceptance of inventory   *176*
最新のグループ会計方針
    latest group accounting policy   *100*
最新のコンタクトリスト
    most up-to-date contact list   *100*

最新のもの
    latest version   *93*
最新の予算
    latest budget   *95*
再テスト
    retest   *177*
再発行する
    reissued   *155*
裁判所
    court   *91*
    tribunal   *91*
差異分析
    variance analysis   *94, 135*
財務活動によるキャッシュ・フロー
    net cash provided by (used in) financing activities
財務状態
    financial position   *74*
財務諸表作成プロセス
    financial statement closing process   *106*
財務制限（条項）
    financial covenant   *119, 161*
財務部
    finance department   *21, 38, 55, 77*
債務不履行
    default   *158*
債務保証
    financial guarantee   *138*
債務免除
    discharge of indebtness   *139*
差異を調整する
    perform the reconciliation   *116*
先入先出法
    first-in first-out method   *170*
先払いの手数料
    up-front fee   *109*
作業分担
    allocation of work   *168*

差入保証金
　guarantee deposits
雑収入（雑損失）
　miscellaneous income（expense）
サブ・プロセス
　sub processes　　*105*
参照ID
　reference ID　　*75*
参照する
　refer to　　*124*
残存価額
　salvage value　　*88*
残高確認
　balance confirmation　　*135*
残高確認状
　confirmation letters　　*11*
暫定契約書
　tentative contract　　*73*
暫定の
　preliminary　　*146*
サンプリング方法
　sampling method　　*175*

し

仕入債務
　payables　　*20*
仕入先
　vendor　　*151*
仕入先コード
　suppliers' code　　*80*
　vendor's code　　*151*
仕入先マスタ
　supplier master　　*81*
仕入先名
　supplier's name　　*80*
仕入帳
　purchase subledger　　*147*
仕入値引
　purchase discount　　*113*

仕入割引
　purchase discount　　*150*
仕掛品
　work in progress　　*178*
時間外手当
　overtime payment　　*88*
時間外労働
　overtime　　*159*
時間給労働者
　part-timers　　*159*
敷金
　rental deposits
識別されたエラー
　errors identified　　*104*
至急
　immediately　　*83, 94, 95, 145*
　Urgent　　*11*
至急対応する
　take immediate action　　*146, 154*
事業価値評価レポート
　the valuation report　　*123*
事業計画
　business plan　　*127*
事業譲渡
　transfer of operation　　*73*
事業撤退損
　loss on business withdrawal
資金繰り表
　cash flow statement　　*117*
資金調達
　financing　　*138*
資金部
　treasury department　　*38*
資金部長
　Treasury manager　　*38*
自己株式
　treasury stock　　*161*
自己株式の取得（処分）
　purchase（disposal）of treasury stock

自己申告（リニエンシー）の申請
application of leniency program　125
資産
asset
資産計上した
capitalized　93
資産取得契約書
Asset Purchase Agreement　10
資産除去債務
asset retirement obligation　13, 136
試算表
trial balance　169
資産評価（PPA）レポート
Purchase Price Allocation (PPA) report　123
指示書
instructions　60
支社別の見積設備投資額
estimated capital expenditure by branch　93
市場価格
market value　136
システム上のデータ
the data in our system　82
システム使用料
IT expense　156
システムでの調整仕訳入力
adjusting entries through system　101
事前許可の要求
any pre-approval requirements　118
事前に
beforehand　159
in advance　147
実効税率
effective income tax rate　132
effective tax rate　100
執行役
executive officer　163
実施する
conduct　90
execute　124
実績
actual results　128
results　94
実践する
implement　139
指定銀行
designated bank　74
指摘する
point out　134
支店
branch　36, 173
支店長
branch manager　20
支払い
payment　83
支払期限
due date　156
payment deadline　144, 153
支払期日
due date　86
payment deadline　146
支払口座
paying account　86
支払催促
demands for payment　156
支払システム
payment system　81
支払条件
payment terms　119
支払処理プロセス
payment process　64
支払超過
overpayment　160
支払手形
notes payable
支払手形明細
detail report of notes payable　155
支払手数料
commission fee

INDEX

193

支払伝票
　disbursement slips　*58*
支払いの実行
　execution of the payment　*83*
支払利息
　interest expense　*130*
四半期決算スケジュール
　quarterly closing schedule　*172*
四半期決算での為替の適用レート一覧表
　list of foreign currencies used for the quarterly closing　*100*
四半期毎
　every quarter　*94*
四半期統制
　quarterly controls　*141*
四半期の決算
　quarter closing　*32, 33*
四半期予算
　quarterly budget　*95*
資本金
　share capital　*74*
資本剰余金
　additional paid-in capital　*74*
資本的支出
　capital expenditures　*158*
社外の専門家
　third party specialist　*91*
社会保険料
　social security expense　*160*
社債
　bonds payable
社債発行
　issuance of corporate bonds　*127*
社債発行費
　bond issuance costs　*114*
社債利息
　interest on bonds
社長
　CEO　*167*
　president　*27*

社内規定
　corporate policies　*138*
社内調査
　in-house investigation　*90*
　internal investigation　*90*
社内便
　interoffice mail　*77*
社内ルール
　internal rules　*158*
車両運搬具
　vehicle　*112*
収益
　revenue
収益認識
　revenue recognition　*33, 34, 170, 172*
収益認識基準
　revenue recognition policy　*33, 65, 98*
従業員
　employee　*163*
修正
　adjustments　*52*
　amendments　*48*
州税
　state tax　*160*
修正後の
　sales order forecast　*66*
修正後目標値
　revised target　*95*
修正された
　revised　*74*
修正仕訳
　adjusting entry　*134*
修正申告書
　amended tax return　*89*
修正する
　amend　*164*
修正予算
　revised budget　*67*
重大なクレーム
　serious complaints　*162*

194

重大な欠陥
    material weaknesses　　104
集団訴訟の訴状
    a class action notice　　123
重要性
    importance　　173
重要な契約の締結
    execution of significant contract　　162
重要な不備
    significant deficiencies　　104
重要な変動
    significant movement　　133
従来
    in the past　　135
従来通り
    As always　　89
主担当者
    be responsible for　　22
受注管理システム
    sales order monitoring system　　66
受注残
    order backlog　　72
受注情報
    order information　　75
受注見込
    revised　　66
出荷
    delivery　　109
出荷基準
    delivery basis　　65
出荷業務
    delivery　　107
出荷数
    number of shipment　　75
出荷報告書
    shipping report　　73, 145
出荷予定日
    scheduled shipping date　　146
出金
    cash disbursements　　158

出金額
    paid amount　　155
出金する
    making the payment　　155
出金伝票
    disbursement slip　　145
    disbursement voucher　　13
出向
    on secondment　　22
出向社員
    secondee　　22
出資
    capital injection　　127
出資金
    investments in capital
出張
    business trip　　15, 40
出張中
    on a business trip　　106
取得
    addition　　158
取得原価
    acquisition cost　　99
主任
    Supervisor　　20, 21
受領書
    delivery report　　149, 152, 178
受領報告書
    customer's acceptance report　　73, 76
仕様
    specification　　153
償却費
    amortization expense　　96
詳細
    details　　17
詳細に
    in detail　　67
使用すべきフォーム
    the forms to be used　　131

195

上長
   supervisor   *60, 66, 75, 142*
承認
   approval   *75*
承認規程
   approval guideline   *158*
承認権限
   approval authority   *23*
証憑
   approval   *76*
   evidence   *67, 176*
   supporting documents   *10*
商標権
   trademarks
商品
   merchandise
商品残高明細
   detail report of inventories   *148*
商品発送
   product shipping   *157*
条文
   Code   *124*
正味実現可能価額
   net realizable value   *135*
賞与
   bonus   *68, 87, 160*
賞与の計算式
   calculation of bonus   *131*
賞与引当金
   accrued bonus   *159*
   bonus provision   *64*
将来加算（減算）一時差異
   future taxable（deductible）temporary difference   *132*
職務経験
   job experiences   *42*
職務権限表
   Delegation of authorization chart   *138*
職務分掌
   segregation of duties   *174*

所得税
   income tax   *160*
処分
   penalty   *163*
仕訳
   journal entries   *64, 114*
仕訳を入力した
   journals were entered   *142*
新会計基準
   newly adopted accounting policy   *170*
新株発行
   issuance of new shares   *127*
人件費
   HR costs   *68*
人件費プロセス
   payroll process   *103*
申告書別表
   schedule   *89*
シンジケーション手数料
   syndication fee   *121*
人事評価
   performance evaluation   *57*
人事部，人事部門
   human resource division   *159*
   human resources department   *49, 174*
迅速なご回答
   prompt response   *15*
迅速に
   promptly   *173*
進捗
   progress   *60, 128*
進捗管理表
   time schedule sheet   *177*
信用枠供与手数料
   arrangement fee   *84*

す

数量
   quantity   *75, 80, 44, 153*

数量差異分析
   quantity variance　*164*
すぐに
   immediately　*131*
スタッフの再教育
   re-education of staff　*168*
ストックオプション
   share-based compensation　*65*
速やかに
   promptly　*162*

せ

税額控除
   tax credit　*137*
正確に
   accurately　*160*
成果報酬
   performance-based fee　*109*
請求金額
   invoice amount　*82*
請求先
   client name on invoice　*144*
請求書
   invoice　*13, 65, 66, 68, 73, 76, 77, 107, 109, 145, 149, 155, 178*
請求書ドラフト
   draft invoice　*78*
請求書の記載内容
   information on the invoice　*113*
請求書の金額
   invoiced amount　*144*
請求書日付
   invoice date　*66*
   date of invoice　*144*
清算計画
   liquidation plan　*127*
精算表
   worksheet　*97*
税制改正
   tax reform

製造部門
   manufacturing department　*174*
製品サンプル
   product sample　*78*
製品の出荷
   shipment of products　*130*
製品別売上
   sales by product　*72*
製品別売上高
   sales by product type　*67*
製品保証引当金
   product warranty provision　*136*
製品ライン別の見積原価
   the estimated cost by product line　*93*
税務上のリスク
   tax related risks　*124*
税務申告書
   tax return　*89*
税務申告書の提出
   filing of tax return　*125*
税務申告書のドラフト
   draft tax return　*97*
税務調査
   tax inspection　*11*
   tax investigation　*124*
税務当局
   tax agency　*115*
   tax authority　*89, 91*
税理士報酬
   tax accountant's fee　*156*
税率
   tax rate　*100*
責任を負う
   be responsible for　*57*
セグメント別の売上高
   sales amount by each segment　*72*
是正措置
   remedial actions　*177*
   your remedial actions　*104*

説明
　explanation　*45, 68*
説明する
　explain　*173*
設立
　incorporation　*127*
前期
　prior year　*103*
前期と当期の差異分析
　analysis of difference between current year balance and prior year balance　*164*
先月までの
　until last month　*94*
先日
　the other day　*140*
全社統制チェックリスト
　company level controls checklist　*106*
　entity level control checklist　*177*
全社統制の不備
　deficiencies in entity level control　*139*
前提条件
　assumptions　*88, 136*
前任者
　fomer in-charge　*24*

そ

増加している
　increased　*132*
総勘定元帳
　general ledger　*68*
早急に
　immediately　*177, 106*
送金
　electronic transfer　*120*
　remittance　*17, 64, 83, 121*
送金限度額
　the remittance limit　*118*
送金手数料
　remittance costs　*86*

送金の目的
　purpose of remittance　*119*
送金振込
　electronic transfer　*117*
増減分析
　fluctuation analysis　*11*
倉庫
　warehouse　*23, 178*
総資産
　total assets　*74*
送付先
　delivery address　*113*
送付方法
　delivery method　*153*
総平均法
　weighted-average method　*170*
組織再編
　reorganization　*12, 39*
組織図
　organization chart　*39, 138*
組織体制
　organization　*39*
組織変更
　change of organization　*38*
訴訟
　lawsuit　*123*
訴訟損失引当金
　provision for loss on litigation
租税条約に関する届出書の提出
　submission of the Income Tax Convention application form　*125*
その他の資産
　other assets　*137*
その他の収益
　other income　*137*
その他の費用
　other expenses　*137*
その他の負債
　other liabilities　*137*

その他包括利益
other comprehensive income
その他有価証券評価差額金
valuation difference on available-for-sale securities
ソフトウェア
software　*79*
ソフトウェア開発委託契約書
Consignment Agreement for Software Development　*11*
ソルベンシーマージン率
solvency margin ratio　*95*
損益計算書
imcome statement　*137, 169*
損金算入費用
tax-deductible expenses　*125*

た

第1四半期
the first-quarter　*72*
対応する
action　*146*
deal with　*154*
take care of it　*161*
代金
payment　*84*
代金の振込み
payment by electronic transfer　*84*
対策
action plan　*95*
measures　*139*
第三者委員会
independent committee　*90*
第三者委員会による不正調査
the fraud investigation by the independent committee　*126*
貸借対照表
balance sheet　*169*
退職給付債務
projected benefit obligation　*88*

退職給付債務の見積り
estmation of projected benefit obligation（PBO）　*131*
退職給付引当金
accrued pension cost　*159*
退職金
retirement allowance　*159*
タイムリー
in a timely manner　*89*
耐用年数
useful life　*136*
滞留
overdue　*109*
滞留在庫のリスト
list of slow-moving inventory　*99*
直ちに
without delay　*151*
タックス・ヘイブン対策税制
Anti-Tax Haven Rules　*115*
立替費用
reimburse for expenses　*85, 154*
例えば
e.g.　*76*
棚卸資産
inventory
棚卸資産の実地棚卸
physical inventory count　*135*
棚卸資産評価
inventory valuation　*13*
棚卸資産評価損
loss on devaluation of inventory　*98*
棚卸資産評価損の計上要件
criteria to record a loss on devaluation of inventory　*98*
単価
unit price　*75, 80, 151*
単価マスタ
unit price master　*81*
短期貸付金
short-term loans receivable　*148*

INDEX

短期借入金
　short-term borrowing　*148*
担当
　operating results　*21*
　be responsible for　*22*
　in-charge　*23*
担当している
　be in-charge of　*23*
担当者
　in-charge　*95*
　person in-charge　*12, 107, 142*
　personnel in-charge　*50*
　responsible personnel　*18*
担当者の交代
　rotation of person in-charge　*168*
担当者名
　contact person　*80*
担保
　mortgage　*154*

ち

チェック体制
　checking procedures　*148*
チェック体制の見直し
　reconsideration of reviewing policy　*168*
チェックマーク
　tick mark　*142*
近い将来
　in the near future　*122*
ちなみに
　By the way　*142*
注意する
　exercise care　*144*
　pay attention　*155*
注記
　footnote　*136*
中期（長期）経営計画
　medium-term (long-term) management plan　*127*

駐在員
　expats　*122*
仲裁人
　arbitrator　*91*
注文
　order　*74, 157*
注文請書
　confirmation of order　*152*
注文書
　order　*149*
　order form　*152*
　purchase order　*13, 77, 155*
　sales order　*73*
注文書のコピー
　copies of sales orders　*76*
注文数量
　order quantity　*74*
長期貸付金
　long-term loans receivable
長期借入金
　long-term debt　*54*
　long-term borrowing　*148*
長期前払費用
　long-term prepaid expenses
長期未払金
　long-term accounts payable - other
調査官
　inspector　*124*
調査する
　investigate　*151*
調整表
　reconciliation schedule　*161*
調達部
　procurement department　*114*
帳簿価額
　book value　*113*
直接費
　direct costs　*129*
賃借料
　rent expense

賃貸契約書
　Lease Agreement　*10*
　Tenancy Agreement　*10*
陳腐化した棚卸資産
　obsolete inventory　*151*

つ

追加テスト
　additional testing　*175*
通常であれば
　normally　*117*
通信費を減らす
　reduce communication expenses　*129*
つまり
　i.e.　*76*

て

提案
　proposal　*42*
提案書
　proposal　*78*
定款
　a copy of Articles of Corporation　*110*
　article of incorporation　*116*
定額法
　straight-line method　*170*
低価法
　lower of cost or market method　*170*
定期預金
　term deposit　*99*
提出
　sales supporting document　*76*
提出期限
　deadline　*104*
定年退職
　retired　*57*
定率法
　declining balance method　*170*
データ・フローチャート
　data flow chart　*102*

適時
　on a timely basis　*162*
適用
　adoption　*172*
適用される
　be in effect　*87*
適用となる
　be effective on　*39*
できるだけ早く
　as soon as possible　*136, 137*
　upon your earliest convenience　*92*
手仕訳
　manual entries　*134*
手数料
　commission　*113*
テスト結果の文書化
　documentation of the test results　*140*
テスト戦略
　testing strategy　*105*
テスト方法
　testing method　*175*
手付金
　deposit　*84*
デモ機
　demo unit　*78*
デューデリジェンスレポート
　due diligence report　*161*
デリバティブ債権
　derivatives
デリバティブ評価益（損）
　gain（Loss）on valuation of derivatives
電子版のフォーム
　e-file form　*89*
電信送金
　electronic transfer　*51*
転送
　transferred　*81*
添付ファイル
　attached file　*53*

電話会議
conference call　26, 32, 45, 94
telecon　25, 28, 30
teleconference　65
telephone conference　27

電話する
make a call　83

と

当期決算の留意事項
key notes for this year's closing　100

当期純利益
net income

当局による調査
investigation by the authority　90

当座貸越の限度額
overdraft limit　119

投資活動によるキャッシュ・フロー
net cash provided by (used in) investing activities

投資と資本の消去仕訳
entries to eliminate investment and capital　134

投資不動産
real estate for investment

当社の請求額
the amount we billed　82

当社予想金額
the amount we expected　82

投資有価証券
investment securities

投資有価証券売却益（損）
gain (loss) on sales of investment securities

投資有価証券評価益（損）
gain (loss) on valuation of investment securities

統制
controls　105

統制テスト
test of controls　103

統制テスト文書
work papers for tests of controls　102

統制にエラーがあった
there was an error on the control　142

統制不備要約表
summary of control deficiencies　104, 177

統制不備要約表の作成
preparation of Summary of Control Deficiencies (SOCD)　140

投入する
launch　129

当年度
current year　54

当年度の
in this fiscal year　94

登録手数料
registration fee　84

得意先
client　151

督促
follow up　109, 117

特別損失
extraordinary expense　137

特別利益
extraordinary income　137

独立企業間価格
prices are at arm's length　115

土地
land

土地再評価差額金
revaluation reserve for land

特許権
patents

特許権使用料の計算書
patent royalty calculation sheet　111

取締役
executive director　43, 163, 167

取締役会
　board of directors meeting　*32, 58, 127*
取締役会議事録
　Board of Directors meeting minutes　*53*
取引
　transaction　*48, 74*
取引価格
　transaction prices　*56*
取引先
　client's／customer's office　*57*
取引条件
　term of business　*74*
取引内容
　transaction conditions　*58*
取引日
　transaction date　*75*
取引日レート
　spot rate　*80, 151*
努力する
　make efforts　*173*

な

内部通報制度
　whistle-blower system　*138*
内部通報制度の有効性
　effectiveness of whistle-blower system　*124*
内部通報の仕組み
　whistle-blower system　*139*
内部統制自己評価
　internal controls self-assessment　*106*
内部統制の不備
　control deficiency　*139*
内部統制の不備に関する改善
　remediation of internal control deficiencies　*11*
内部取引一覧表
　list of intercompany transactions　*97*

内部の財務報告
　internal financial reporting　*20*
内容
　description　*141*
何らかの書類の提出要求
　any document requirements　*118*

に

日次統制
　daily controls　*141*
日米租税条約
　Japan-U.S. Tax Treaty　*115*
日系企業
　Japanese companies　*161*
入金
　cash receipts　*158*
　payment　*85*
入金遅延
　delayed payment　*157*
入金伝票
　receiving slip　*145*
入手予定日
　target date　*91*
入力が漏れている箇所
　missing fields　*165*
入力ミス
　typing error　*165*

ね

値引
　discount　*150*
年間EBITDA予測
　annual EBITDA forecast　*93*
年間目標値
　annual target　*95*
年金数理人
　actuary　*91*
年次統制
　annual controls　*141*

年２回
    semi-annually   *135*
念のための確認ですが
    Just to clarify   *120*
年末賞与
    year-end bonus   *56*
年齢表
    aging list   *144*

の

納入期限
    delivery deadline   *146, 153*
納品書
    delivery report   *155*
    delivery slip   *77, 112*
残りの
    remaining   *84*
のれん
    goodwill
のれんの減損テスト
    impairment test of goodwill   *135*

は

売却可能有価証券
    available-for-sale securities
配送先住所
    delivery address   *74*
配属
    be assigned to   *22*
派遣社員
    temporary workers   *160*
破産更生債権等
    claims provable in bankruptcy, claims provable in rehabilitation and other
発注先の住所
    vendor address   *113*
発注数量
    order quantity   *113*
発注単価
    unit price   *113*

払込資本金
    paid-in capital
払戻の請求
    claim for refund   *83*
半期統制
    semi annual controls   *141*
半期予算
    half year budget   *93*
販促費
    promotional costs   *96*
販売インセンティブ
    sales incentive   *144*
販売管理システム
    sales management system   *108*
販売計画
    sales plan   *96*
販売システム
    sales system   *75, 174*
販売システムと会計システムの自動連携
    automated coordination of sales system and accounting system   *139*
販売実績
    sales performance   *75*
販売手数料
    sales commission   *150*
販売費および一般管理費
    selling, general and administrative expenses   *130*
販売予測
    sales forecast   *72, 95*

ひ

比較
    comparison   *72*
非課税取引
    non-taxable transaction   *176*
引当金
    allowance   *87*
    provision   *67, 114*

引当金明細表
　breakdown of provisions　99
引受人
　underwriter　91
引き継ぐ
　be taking over　22
　handover　38
　take over　38, 39
引き続き注意する
　keep an eye on this　153
被告
　defendant　91
ビジネスの実務
　business practices　112
日付
　date　80
必要であれば
　if necessary　154
必要なエビデンスの種類
　type of evidence required　98
必要な承認権限
　necessary authorization　167
必要な対応
　necessany steps　149
備品
　equipment　79
評価益（損）
　revaluation gain (loss)
評価性引当金
　valuation allowance　100
評価レポート
　valuation report　178
表示方法
　disclosure policy　171
標準原価
　standard costing　81
品質
　quality　153

ふ

ファイナンス・リース
　finance lease　73
付加価値税
　value-added tax (VAT)　130
複雑な
　complicated　168
福利厚生費
　welfare expense　88, 166
負債
　debt
負債資本比率
　debt to equity ratio　127
不自然な変動
　unusual fluctuations　166
付随費用
　incidental costs
不正
　illegal act　163
不正行為
　fraud　162
　fraudulent activities　90
不正の再発防止策
　measures to prevent recurrence/
　reoccurrence of fraud　124
付属文書
　addendum　108
部長
　Manager, Corrtroller　20
物流
　logistic　79
物流部門
　logistics department　178
不動産鑑定評価書
　real estate appraisal report　161
不動産売買契約書
　Purchase and Sale Agreement of Real Estate　10

INDEX

205

船荷証券
　bill of lading　*178*
不備
　deficiency　*177*
部門予算
　department budget　*96*
フリーキャッシュフローの計算方法
　calculation method of Free Cash Flow
　（FCF）　*131*
振替伝票
　journal entry slip　*145*
振込み
　bank transfer　*85*
振込む
　transfer　*84*
不良債権
　bad debts　*148*
不良在庫
　goods impaired by damage/
　deterioration　*148*
プレスリリース
　press release　*59*
フローチャート
　flow chart　*102, 141*
プロセス・オーナー
　process owner　*105*
粉飾決算
　window dressing　*124*
分析
　analysis　*100*
分析する
　analyze　*130*
分納1回目の支払い
　first installment payment　*85*

へ

米国会計基準
　US-GAAP　*170*
別掲項目
　separate line item　*171*

ヘッジ会計
　hedge accounting　*114*
返金
　refund　*85, 158*
弁護士の見解
　a legal opinion　*123*
弁護士報酬
　attorney's fee　*156*
返済
　repayment　*117*
変動費
　variable costs　*93*
返品
　sales return　*150*
返品関連証憑
　evidence relating to sales return　*76*
返品権
　right of return　*108*
返品処理
　sales returns　*107*
返品数量
　number of goods returned　*116*
返品引当金
　sales return provision　*136*

ほ

包括利益
　comprehensive income
報告期限
　reporting deadline　*98*
報告書日
　reporting date　*172*
方策
　measures　*129*
法人税申告書作成
　preparation of corporate tax return
　20
法人税の申告期限延長申請書
　application for extension of time to file
　corporate income tax　*89*

法定監査の監査報告書
 audit report of statutory audit *169*
法定耐用年数
 statutory useful life *151*
法務部
 legal department *73, 90, 91*
法律事務所による法務デューデリジェンス
 the legal Due Diligence procedures by the law firm *126*
法律上の制限
 legal restrictions *118*
法令順守に関する従業員調査
 employee survey on compliance *90*
保管
 storage *79*
保管する
 store *150*
保管方法
 storage method *178*
保守的な
 conservative *129*
保証金
 guarantee deposit *84*
保証債務
 guarantee obligation
補助簿
 sub ledger *68*
補足帳票
 supplementary schedules *97*
本社
 head office *21, 22, 101*
 headquarters *12, 16, 22, 41, 44, 52, 56, 57*
本社経理部
 headquarters accounting department *46*
本社経理部への問い合わせ
 questions to the accounting department *101*

本部長
 General Manager *20, 30, 59, 106, 167*

ま

前受金
 advances received
前受収益
 unearned revenue
前に
 previously *161*
前払金
 advance payments
前払費用
 prepaid expense
間に合う
 in time *178*
マニュアル統制のテスト
 test of manual controls *103*
マネジメントアカウント
 management accounts *45*

み

未経過利息
 unearned interest *137*
未検収の商品
 unaccepted goods *170*
未実現利益消去仕訳
 entries to eliminate unrealized profit *134*
未収収益
 accrued income
未収入金
 other account receivable *154*
未収配当金
 dividend receivable *157*
未着品
 goods in-transit *112*
 undelivered goods *109*
見積り
 estimate *77*

forecasted　*66*
quotation　*157*

見積コスト
estimated cost　*162*

見積書
quotation　*66, 78, 152*
quote　*112*
sales quote　*73, 144*

見積書の内容
contents of the quotation　*108*

見直す
re-examine　*105*
reassess　*152, 178*
reconsider　*148, 158*

未払金
accounts payable　*112*

未払配当金
dividend payable

未払費用
accrued expense　*114*

未払利息
accrued interest　*121*

む

無形資産
intangible assets　*132*

無形資産の評価レポート
valuation report of intangible asset　*161*

め

明確にする
clarify　*174*

明細
breakdown　*93*

メール
by email　*169*

免除
exemptions　*118*

免税取引
tax exempt transaction　*176*

も

目的
purpose　*118*

目論見書
offering circular　*161*

もし必要であれば
if necessary　*100*

持株会社
holding company　*106*

持分法
equity method　*114*

元従業員
former employee　*163*

や

役員報酬
directors' compensation　*87*

約束手形の明細
breakdown of promissory note　*148*

ゆ

有価証券
investment securities　*24*

有価証券時価情報
market price information of security　*161*

有価証券売却益（損）
gain（loss）on sales of securities

有価証券評価益（損）
gain（loss）from revaluation of investment securities

有給休暇引当金
in accrued vacation payable　*132*
vacation accrual　*88*

遊休資産
long-lived assets temporarily idled　*99*

有形固定資産
 Property, Plant and Equipment
有形固定資産残高
 balance in Property, Plant and Equipment (PP&E)　*132*
有形固定資産の評価
 PP&E evaluation　*126*
融資限度額
 line of credit　*119, 157*
有利子負債
 interest bearing debt　*95*

よ

翌年度
 following year　*134*
予算
 budget　*56, 66, 92, 94, 169*
予算案
 budget plan　*127*
予算会議
 budget meeting　*12*
予算システムへの入力
 input to budget system　*164*
予算実績管理
 monitoring of budget against actual　*11*
予算実績分析
 budget-actual analysis　*164*
予算達成率
 achievement rate against your target budget　*95*
予算と実績の差異分析
 analysis of the difference between budget and actual figures　*164*
予算を下回っている
 below the budget target　*130*
与信限度額
 credit limit　*74, 108*

ら

来期
 next fiscal year　*138*
来月の頭
 beginning of next month　*100*
来週の金曜までに
 by next Friday　*92*
ライセンス契約書
 License Agreement　*10*
来年度
 next fiscal year　*131*

り

リース資産（債務）
 lease assets (obligation)　*99*
利益計画
 profit planning　*76*
利益準備金
 legal reserve
利益剰余金
 retained earning　*74*
利益操作
 manipulation　*105*
リスク管理規程
 Risk Management Policy　*138*
リスク・コントロール・マトリクス
 risk control matrix　*102*
リスク・フリー・レート
 risk free rate　*121*
リストラ引当金
 restructuring provision　*136*
利息費用
 interest expense　*129*
リベート
 rebate　*109, 150*
リマインド
 Reminder　*11*
理由
 explanation　*89*

留意事項
　concerns　17
流動資産
　current asset　148
流動比率
　current ratio　127
流動負債
　current liability　148
領収書
　receipt　77
旅費交通費
　travel expense　166
旅費交通費を減らす
　reduce travel expenses　129
稟議書
　Ringi (circular letter)　112

れ

レビュー統制
　review controls　103
レポーティングパッケージ
　reporting package　32, 67, 131
レポーティングパッケージの作成
　input to reporting package　164
レポーティングパッケージの送付先
　addressee of the reporting package　131
連結会計システム
　consolidation accounting system　36
連結決算
　consolidation closing　43
連結決算スケジュール
　closing schedule　12
連結決算帳票
　consolidation reporting package　10, 11, 13

連結子会社
　consolidated subsidiary　12
連結システムの操作方法に関する一般的な質問
　general questions about how to operate the consolidation system　101
連結システムへの入力
　entries to the consolidation system　101
連結消去仕訳
　consolidation elimination entries　134
連結パッケージ
　consolidation package　52
　reporting package　97, 169
連動している
　linked　81
連絡先担当者
　contact person　98
連絡窓口
　contact　22

ろ

ロイヤルティ契約書
　Royalty Agreement　10
労働者派遣契約書
　Worker Dispatch Agreement　11
労務費用
　labor costs

わ

和解提案
　a settlement proposal　123
割引率
　discount rate　65
割引率の見直し
　revision of discount rate

【執筆者・監修】

＜執筆者＞

田村　浩一（新日本有限責任監査法人　品質管理本部　キャピタルマーケッツ部　マネージャー）

本山　禎晃（同　第3事業部　マネージャー）

齋藤　圭佑（同　第3事業部　マネージャー）

越智　洋平（同　第3事業部　マネージャー）

加藤　典子（同　第3事業部　シニア）

佐藤　一（同　第3事業部　シニア）

村井　隆紘（同　金融事業部　シニア）

岡田　紳一郎（同　第5事業部　シニア）

若林　真喜子（同　第3事業部　シニア）

飯村　桂子（同　金融部　シニア）

古川　詩野（同　金融アドバイザリー部　スタッフ）

稲葉　由衣（同　第1事業部　アソシエート）

＜監修＞

中川　政人（新日本有限責任監査法人　第5事業部　シニアパートナー）

デーブ・ディクソン（同　品質管理本部　キャピタルマーケッツ部　パートナー）

ポール・サーストン（同　品質管理本部　キャピタルマーケッツ部　パートナー）

スコット・ウォーカー（同　品質管理本部　キャピタルマーケッツ部　パートナー）

スティーブ・トゥッカー（同　第2事業部　パートナー）

中村　美由樹（同　第2事業部　パートナー）

沢木　ニコラ（同　品質管理本部　IFRSデスク　シニアプリンシパル）

アンドリュー・カウエル（同　企画マーケッツ本部　推進部　エグゼクティブ・ディレクター）

【編者紹介】

EY | Assurance | Tax | Transactions | Advisory

新日本有限責任監査法人について
新日本有限責任監査法人は，EYメンバーファームです。全国に拠点を持つ日本最大級の監査法人業界のリーダーです。監査および保証業務をはじめ，各種財務アドバイザリーの分野で高品質なサービスを提供しています。EYグローバルネットワークを通じ，日本を取り巻く経済活動の基盤に信頼をもたらし，より良い社会の構築に貢献します。詳しくは，www.shinnihon.or.jpをご覧ください。

EYについて
EYは，アシュアランス，税務，トランザクションおよびアドバイザリーなどの分野における世界的なリーダーです。私たちの深い洞察と高品質なサービスは，世界中の資本市場や経済活動に信頼をもたらします。私たちはさまざまなステークホルダーの期待に応えるチームを率いるリーダーを生み出していきます。そうすることで，構成員，クライアント，そして地域社会のために，より良い社会の構築に貢献します。

EYとは，アーンスト・アンド・ヤング・グローバル・リミテッドのグローバルネットワークであり，単体，もしくは複数のメンバーファームを指し，各メンバーファームは法的に独立した組織です。アーンスト・アンド・ヤング・グローバル・リミテッドは，英国の保証有限責任会社であり，顧客サービスは提供していません。詳しくは，ey.comをご覧ください。

本書は一般的な参考情報の提供のみを目的に作成されており，会計，税務およびその他の専門的なアドバイスを行うものではありません。新日本有限責任監査法人および他のEYメンバーファームは，皆様が本書を利用したことにより被ったいかなる損害についても，一切の責任を負いません。具体的なアドバイスが必要な場合は，個別に専門家にご相談ください。

そのまま使える　経理の英文メール

2015年12月15日　第1版第1刷発行
2025年4月10日　第1版第14刷発行

編　者　新日本有限責任監査法人
発行者　山　本　　継
発行所　㈱中央経済社
発売元　㈱中央経済グループ
　　　　パブリッシング

〒101-0051　東京都千代田区神田神保町1-35
　　　　　　電話　03（3293）3371（編集代表）
　　　　　　　　　03（3293）3381（営業代表）
　　　　　　https://www.chuokeizai.co.jp
　　　　　　印刷・製本／昭和情報プロセス㈱

©2015 Ernst & Young ShinNihon LLC.
All Rights Reserved.
Printed in Japan

＊頁の「欠落」や「順序違い」などがありましたらお取り替えいたしますので発売元までご送付ください。（送料小社負担）
ISBN978-4-502-16581-8　C3034

JCOPY〈出版者著作権管理機構委託出版物〉本書を無断で複写複製（コピー）することは，著作権法上の例外を除き，禁じられています。本書をコピーされる場合は事前に出版者著作権管理機構（JCOPY）の許諾を受けてください。
　JCOPY〈https://www.jcopy.or.jp　eメール：info@jcopy.or.jp〉

一目でわかるビジュアルガイド

図解でざっくり会計シリーズ　全8巻

新日本有限責任監査法人 [編]　　　　各巻1,900円＋税

本シリーズの特徴
- ■シリーズキャラクター「ざっくり君」がやさしくナビゲート
- ■コンセプトは「図とイラストで理解できる」
- ■原則，1テーマ見開き
- ■専門用語はできるだけ使わずに解説
- ■重要用語はKeywordとして解説
- ■「ちょっと難しい」プラスαな内容はOnemoreとして解説

1	税効果会計のしくみ	5つのステップでわかりやすく解説。連結納税制度や組織再編，資産除去債務など，税効果に関係する特殊論点についてもひと通り網羅。
2	退職給付会計のしくみ	特有の用語をまとめた用語集付き。改正退職給付会計基準もフォロー。
3	金融商品会計のしくみ	ますます複雑になる重要分野を「金融資産」，「金融負債」，「デリバティブ取引」に分けて解説。
4	減損会計のしくみ	減損会計の概念を携帯電話会社を例にしたケーススタディ方式でやさしく解説。
5	連結会計のしくみ	のれん・非支配株主持分・持分法などの用語アレルギーを感じさせないように，連結決算の基礎をやさしく解説。
6	キャッシュ・フロー計算書のしくみ	どこからお金が入り，何に使ったのか，「会社版お小遣い帳」ともいえる計算書のしくみを解説。
7	組織再編会計のしくみ	各章のはじめに組織再編の全体像を明示しながら解説。組織再編の類型や適用される会計基準，さらに各手法の比較まで言及。
8	リース会計のしくみ	リース取引のしくみや，資産計上するときの金額の算定方法等，わかりやすく解説。特有の用語集付。

■中央経済社■